819.6   Tivy, Louis.
Tivy   Your loving Anna; letters from the
          Ontario frontier. Toronto, University of
          Toronto Press, 1972.
             120 p. illus., maps.

RELATED
BOOKS IN
CATALOG   1. Leveridge, Anna.   I. Title.
UNDER

                                    (72-86392)
                                     G-8878

your loving Anna

LETTERS FROM THE ONTARIO FRONTIER

your loving Anna

LETTERS FROM THE ONTARIO FRONTIER

LOUIS TIVY

University of Toronto Press

© University of Toronto Press 1972
Printed in Canada
ISBN 0-8020-1927-7 (Cloth)
ISBN 0-8020-6166-4 (Paper)
Microfiche ISBN 0-8020-0263-3
LC 72-86392

PUBLISHER'S NOTE

Louis Tivy, who prepared the letters of Anna Leveridge for publication and wrote the accompanying text, was Anna's grandson. He
seems to have resembled her in many ways – in love of nature, cour-
age in adversity, faith, and friendship. He died in January 1972,
shortly after this book had been accepted for publication. Verna
Tivy, his widow, has written the brief account of his life which follows.

Anna Leveridge's letters were not altered by her editor except to
punctuate and paragraph them, for, doubtless to save space (and postage), Anna ran sentences together and seldom used paragraphs. There
was no need to correct her spelling or grammar, which were practi-
cally perfect.

In writing the accompanying text, Louis Tivy drew upon the recol-
lections of his grandparents, and memories of his own childhood in
rural Ontario. There is a remarkable identity of feeling and tone between Anna's letters and his text.

Neither the letters nor the text deal with great events, nor with as-
pects of pioneer life hitherto unknown, but they have the ring of
truth that is to be found only in first-hand accounts, and they bring
us closer to those who lived here in early times.

To my grandmother

ANNA LEVERIDGE

who brought her children from England to make a home with
her husband in the backwoods of Hastings County. She learned
to live frugally, making no complaint about doing without many
things she had once regarded as necessities. She devoted her life
to improving her surroundings, helping her neighbours, and, seeing beyond disappointments, ever counting her blessings and
strengthening her faith in God.

LOUIS TIVY

Louis was born in 1902 on the farm where his grandparents, David and Anna Leveridge, lived. When he was six years old, his father died following a kick by a horse. His mother was left with three boys and baby girl, the eldest son only eight years of age.

Louis developed polio in childhood. As a result he walked with a limp all his life. I once heard him say that because he walked slower than others, he had time to learn and to be observant.

He was educated in the little country school about two and one-half miles from his home, walking both ways each day, and I am sure it must have been very difficult in the winter. He was able to go to high school for just one year in Bancroft, and the rest of his education he received by studying at night and taking summer courses.

He was first a teacher in a country school, within walking distance of his home, for I know he walked home on the weekends. He taught at various schools for about seven years, before moving to the northern part of Ontario, where he spent five years at Hearst and ten at Cochrane. While in Cochrane he became interested in manual training, and began to teach it. It was at Cochrane that we met; I was a teacher on the same staff and in many ways he made things easier for me.

He left the north in 1945 and began to teach manual training in Leamington District High School. When he started he was the only teacher in the shop department; when he retired, twenty years later, he headed a staff of six.

Just before his retirement, he suffered a heart attack. Upon recovery, he turned to writing, and spent many hours doing just that. His articles, dealing with nature or with pioneer days, were published in the *Family Herald*, and the Leamington *Post and News*. I have heard him say that he always wanted to write, but after a full day at school was too tired.

He loved flowers, trees, and the birds, and had a way with all of them. He often visited the Grade One classes I taught in the local school, and always came with a treat and a story. Many of the local young people remember Louis's visits.

The only dislikes I knew him to have were cats, new clothes, and sauerkraut.

VERNA TIVY

your loving Anna

LETTERS FROM THE ONTARIO FRONTIER

THE LEVERIDGE FAMILY

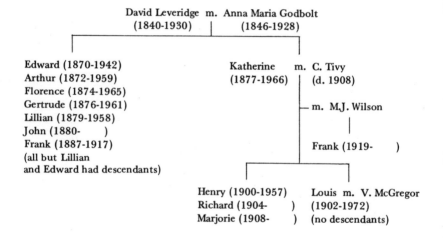

David Leveridge m. Anna Maria Godbolt
(1840-1930) | (1846-1928)

Edward (1870-1942)   Katherine   m. C. Tivy
Arthur (1872-1959)   (1877-1966) | (d. 1908)
Florence (1874-1965)
Gertrude (1876-1961)   — m. M.J. Wilson
Lillian (1879-1958)
John (1880-   )   Frank (1919-   )
Frank (1887-1917)
(all but Lillian
and Edward had descendants)

              Henry (1900-1957)   Louis m. V. McGregor
              Richard (1904-   )   (1902-1972)
              Marjorie (1908-   ) (no descendants)

1

Hastings county in southern Ontario extends a long, probing finger northwards, reaching from the gently rolling fertile farmlands that surround the Bay of Quinte far back into the forested highlands at the lower edge of the Laurentian shield. The Loyalist settlers, who came to the district following the American revolution, stayed mainly on the bay and along the shores of Lake Ontario, where lay better and more level lands. Later comers had to venture farther into the backwoods where cheaper land was still available.

Nestled in these backwoods, areas of good land were still often to be found, ringed about by hills that grew ever higher the farther the homeseekers advanced. The newcomers followed in the footsteps of the exploring surveyors, improving their rough trails into crude early roads. The settlers homesteaded the fertile pockets, forming tiny settlements that later became less remote when the railway poked up into the wilderness. The railway was built originally to gain access to the stands of giant white pines interspersed among the hardwood forests, but it also served for many years to link small communities to larger centres such as Trenton and Belleville "out Front," as the southern edge of the county was called.

Most of the early settlers were farmers intent on owning their own piece of land, clearing their own fields, accumulating their own livestock, and living mainly on products of their own raising. Money was scarce; good jobs meant spending long periods away from home where work was to be had at logging camps or in railway building.

Walking was the most common means of getting about and of carrying goods, but a yoke of oxen was added as soon as possible to the meagre list of settlers' equipment. People lived as close together as they could, for neighbours were valuable, helping each other with heavy jobs, and sharing the amusements which the settlers had to make for themselves. Most were equally poor in worldly goods, so all were happier together.

Communications with the outside world were spotty and irregular. Newspapers and periodicals were infrequent and were passed from home to home as long as they were legible. Weeks or months elapsed before important news reached outlying settlements.

Sunday was a day of rest from the labours of the week. People gathered at church meetings as much to trade local gossip as to worship; often they had no regular minister. Schools were scarce, and attending one was a privilege limited largely to those too young to be of any real help on the farm.

Newcomers were welcomed. This was especially true for those talented in any way that would add to the entertainment of groups that met on special occasions. Anyone able to sing, play an instrument, or tell a good story was received warmly into the community.

Some of the immigrants adapted more readily than others to pioneer conditions. They accepted the temporary privations of their new life, made themselves happy with what they had, and looked forward to the future instead of grieving over a way of life that was gone. Such persons were valued highly. They were sought out for the uplift in spirits gained by contact with the cheerful sureness of their trust that life must grow better in God's good time. Their faith was contagious and lighted candles of hope to shine through troubled lives.

One of these strong personalities was Anna Leveridge. She had been torn rudely from her English home of comfort and plenty and dropped on a backwoods farm among a group of pioneers. There, her faith and unfailing cheer brightened the lives of those among whom she moved.

While her mother in England lived, Anna wrote long letters home to describe her new way of life. No complaints were made of the hardships she endured. Her letters painted pictures of early Canada for her parents. Fortunately, they have been preserved and form a record of pioneer times in North Hastings county.

David Leveridge and his family joined the flow of immigrants to Canada in the early 1880s. His story was similar to that of many other newcomers. David had been overseer of Park Farm, an estate in Hochering near Norwich in eastern England. He and his wife Anna, with their family of six children, lived in a rambling country home on the estate; a house so large that according to family tradition, occasionally they would move to a different set of rooms, just for a change.

Anna was organist in the parish church. The family grew up with a steady faith in God, a faith strengthened by daily family worship. Life appeared good, and seemed secure. They enjoyed many comforts: food in plenty; good clothing, for Anna was clever with her sewing machine; education; a well-rounded way of life. David rode a good horse about the farmlands to direct operations at each season.

Even at Hochering there were, of course, some rumblings of discontent. In the evening gatherings at the village pub, tall tales were told of the money this or that person had made after braving emigration to one of the colonies. One evening it was Australia, another time Canada, and next time New Zealand that shone in the rosy hues common to far-off places.

Life for the family might well have gone on indefinitely in this pattern. But David, whose nature was trusting and generous, backed a friend's note for a considerable sum. His faith in the honesty of his friend was betrayed. The man vanished, the money with him. Laws were severe concerning money matters in England; those who couldn't pay their debts went to prison. David had no choice other than paying the note in full when it became due. This took everything he had.

The blow to the family was heavy; their savings were now gone and their future uncertain. Security had disappeared over night. Facing them were long years of struggle and hard work to replace even a part of what was lost.

David became depressed in spirits beyond the ability of Anna's cheerfulness to cure. He felt bitterly that his negligence and too ready trust had hurt his family, and he was ashamed to face his friends. The idea of emigration to one of the colonies in order to start over again among new faces became insistent in his mind. But he did not discuss the matter with Anna; if he had, the outcome might have been different. When he could stand the situation no longer, he did not even bid goodbye to his family and friends, but disappeared.

Anna found no explanation on the morning after his departure. No one had seen him go. True, he had talked, as had others in the neighbourhood, about leaving for one of the colonies to try gathering some of the easy money to be found there, but days passed with no message. At last, after a week or so, there came a brief note from him. It said only that he was on his way to Canada, and that they would hear from him later.

Weeks passed, and the time grew into months. Anna lay awake many nights, reviewing her hopes and fears. She hadn't told David that a new baby was on its way. She had to plan to provide for it and for the family herself. Her playing of the church organ took on a new meaning. The pay for that service, with what she earned from giving music lessons and her skill as a seamstress, kept the family together. Her sewing machine was seldom idle in any spare time that she could find from housekeeping. The children learned to help whenever they could.

Anna prayed often for help and guidance. Slowly, out of this soul-searching, grew sure faith that things would yet work out for the best. David would manage. He would return and they would make their lives anew. But David never saw England again.

As David's ship sailed day after day up the mighty St. Lawrence, he was vastly impressed by the great expanse of Canada. He watched with eager interest when they stopped in Quebec to unload part of the cargo. The passengers found it good to get on shore for a few hours although the firm earth underfoot seemed for a while to roll gently as the ship's deck had done for the past weeks.

The rapid chatter of French sounded strange to David's ears. Not understanding, it repelled him, although he found the buildings quaint and was fascinated by everything he saw. But the steep streets leading up the cliff to the citadel, the shouts, the smells, the towering hills in the distance, were not what he had come to find. This was not the place he had visioned in his mind when he started from home. It wasn't for him.

The ship finally docked in Montreal, ending the sea part of his journey. Now David was on his own. He found Montreal, too, a busy place, unlike the peaceful countryside he had left. Hearing of English-speaking settlements farther to the west, he left by train, heading for the Bay of Quinte where he thought he might find settlers more like himself.

Belleville even then was a busy town beautifully situated at the mouth of the Moira river between low rolling hills. He liked the place at once, and it was homelike to hear English spoken. Here surely money could be made. But honest fortunes are hard to come by. David learned that without special training or some capital to invest he had little to offer a prospective employer. Heavy work as a labourer he could have in plenty, but he was not accustomed to it. In his search for jobs he drifted away from the city into the farmlands of the northern and newer areas. There he found occasional work, but was able to save very little. He put off writing home to Anna, because as yet he had no fixed address where he could count on staying long enough to receive a reply.

In the country near Madoc small pockets of gold nuggets had been found in the rocky outcroppings. He was fascinated by these discoveries, dreaming of becoming suddenly rich through finding minerals – a lure that he never forgot. The hills and rocks became a challenge.

Ever searching for a likely place to settle, David came to Millbridge. Here there was plenty of hard work, for a railway line was being pushed into the wilderness of the northern part of Hastings county. It would give access to the stands of white pine timber through that region as well as connect small and isolated groups of settlers with the larger centres in the south. David saw that the land was becoming poorer for farming as he went farther into the north, but still there were fertile pockets of tillable soil among the ever higher hills. The thought of mineral wealth possibly lying underground waiting to be found led him on.

For some months David stayed in the settlement at Millbridge and here winter caught up with him. Fellow workers had told him at great length about the intense cold and deep snows of that Canadian season but their stories seemed so much exaggerated that he couldn't believe them. Being ill prepared, he caught cold, refused to lay off work, and became quite sick. Kindly people tried to help him, but by the time he recovered and could return to work his small savings were almost used up.

Depressed in spirits anew, lonely and needing comfort, he decided that it was time to write to Anna, even though he had little money to send her. Perhaps she, in one of her mysterious ways, would be able to gather enough for the family to come and join him. At least, they could be together again and surely would manage somehow. In spite of the troubles he had had in this new land, it seemed to him a good place to raise a family. Eddie and Arthur, his oldest boys, aged 11 and 10, would delight in the Canadian way of life, would be fascinated with the outdoors, and soon adapt to the surroundings. So the letter was written and mailed.

A burden lifted from his mind, he soon grew less lonely, and worked with new vigour to be ready for his family's arrival, never doubting that Anna would come. She would contrive. With the family together again, all would go better. People always liked Anna, and this would make a real difference in how they got along. Compared with the big house in Hochering, accommodations might be rough at first, but they would soon build a home of their own.

Each week David walked the few extra miles to the post office, thinking that an answer might come from Anna. He had grown accustomed to the bitter wintry days and was now dressed to suit the weather. His muscles hardened and his body strengthened so that the heavy work seemed no longer tough to master.

9

He could now swing an axe or handle a shovel along with the best of the men in the gang, and he earned the respect of those around him.

4

At home in England, Anna and the family had been having difficulties too. They had soon used up the supplies that were in the house when David left, and although everyone had begun to learn to do without many things, it became increasingly hard to make ends meet. The money Anna received as church organist and from her music pupils seemed to disappear like magic. Her sewing kept her busy but brought very small returns. There were so many places to put every penny and so few pennies to put in them. The children were too small to work, and opportunities for Eddie and Arthur were too few for them to earn very much to help out. Before long there would be a new little one to care for, which added to Anna's worries.

As the time passed, Anna began to feel as though she were being separated from the familiar things around her. Without David, much of the brightness went from her life. Her desire to be with him again began to outweigh her love for the life they had known in England together. Others lived in those newer lands and made homes there, perhaps God intended her family to do the same.

Late in the autumn, David's letter arrived. The sight of his handwriting on the envelope brought sudden tears of relief. She skimmed hurriedly over the familiar expressions of regard and the greetings, absorbing the important details first. Many later readings would fill in and glean the minor items. Her feelings

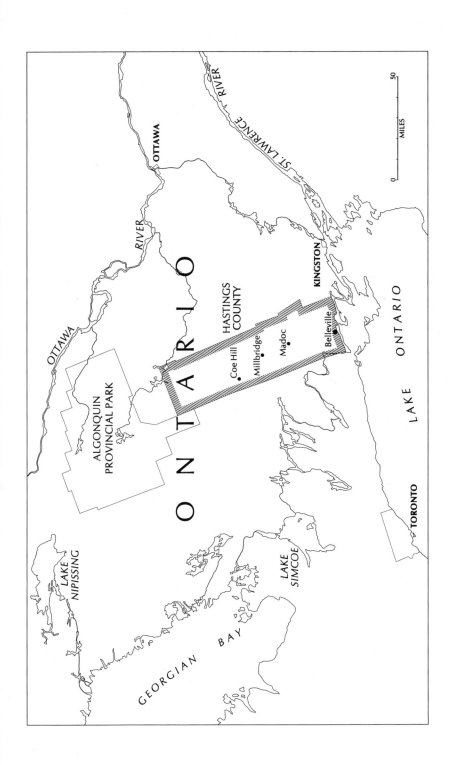

were mixed. She was relieved that the long suspense of not hearing from him had ended. She was interested in how he had lived, and troubled about his illness. The idea of going to meet him in Canada was not a real surprise. But the letter brought fresh problems. With so little help from him, how could she assemble the passage money? What should they try to take with them? When should she plan on leaving? Certainly it couldn't be soon for the new baby was nearly due, and winter coming on. She had much to decide, and each decision was important.

Anna wrote at once to her mother who lived a few miles away in a neighbouring village. This was her letter:

Hochering/E. Dereham

My dearest Mother and all

I know you are looking out for a letter from me. I had one from David yesterday but no money. He has been ill and out of work, as you will see by his letter which I will enclose, then you can return it.

What I am to do, I don't know. Mr. A. came in yesterday. He is going to see what he can get for the watch as I must have some money. He let me have another 10/. He is very kind.

You will see David wants us to go almost directly, but I have just been writing to him to say I cannot see how it is to be done, as he cannot send me any money. Of course, if he has been ill he could not do so, but I tell him if I have to sell my things to live, how am I to raise sufficient money to take us away? I know his thought is that the things will make enough, and so perhaps they would, if I could have kept the money for that. But as it is, I don't see how I can go yet for a few weeks at any rate, do you?

I hope you are pretty well. We are the same, thank God. I have a good many friends. Fanny Milk sent me $\frac{1}{2}$ pt. of butter, $\frac{1}{2}$ score eggs, and a piece of meat this morning. John Leveridge has set up butchering two weeks. He sent me enough meat to last for three days, which was a great treat, besides some suet. Not being able to pay my way bothers me very much, but it is not my fault, and the Lord will provide, no doubt, though things look black. Still, there is a silver lining which will be seen soon no doubt.

Excuse more now. Love to Mary and Father and all, not forgetting yourself.

Anna

When Anna heard from David again, he agreed that she should wait till early in the summer before leaving for Canada. By then she would be strong again after the birth of her child and would have time to decide what to take with her.

The delay made it possible for David to send much of the passage money, and help came from other sources. When the amount was safely in her keeping, Anna gave a thankful sigh of relief. Her faith had been justified. When God had closed the door on her past way of life, he had opened another; and now she was able to see the new path clear before her.

In the early summer of 1883 Anna wrote a hurried note to her mother from the ship before it carried her away from England.

Dearest Mother and all

On board all right and children and luggage. A large ship, crowded with people. We have got a berth to ourselves. Found a gentleman who helped us with everything, so kind. So is everybody. Plenty to pay, though, this way and that. Let the others know, as the tug is now going to leave. Love to all and farewells. Children are happy.

It has been a fight, but "the Lord fought for us, and we held our peace." Thanks be to his Holy Name. Goodbye. Love and kisses. [Will] write again as soon as we can.

[Anna]

The tug dropped its lines. The gap widened. England began to drop behind. While all eyes were fastened on the receding shores, suddenly their minds were taken from the farewell scene.

"Where's Eddie?" asked Arthur of the little group huddled against the rail.

A quick search revealed no small boy on the deck, nor any sign of his familiar, tousled head of hair. This alarm immediately replaced their sadness at leaving. A thorough search was organized by the passengers for the young lad; most of the sailors were busy at duties connected with leaving port and could give little help.

It was nearly an hour before Eddie was found by his distracted family. He had been eager to learn exactly how this mighty ship was driven through the waters, and had quietly made his way down to the boiler room. There he had watched the huge engines spring into life and the propellor shaft begin its revolutions that would not cease till anchor was dropped in Canadian waters.

By the time all was serene again in the Leveridge family, a cloud of mist on the horizon was all that marked the spot where England had been. Then came the job of stowing the luggage neatly into the confined area of their berth, the tiny space that they would occupy during the week or more that the passage would take. Perhaps the smallness of their living quarters was an indication of the new conditions to confront them in the days and years ahead.

The eleventh of July, 1883, dawned bright and clear in Hastings county, with a light breeze blowing from the southwest. Before daylight David had set out for Madoc with a borrowed team of horses and light waggon. When the sun came up rosily over the hills, his spirits soared with it. Surely this day would mark the start of happier times for his family.

For Anna and the children it meant the end of long months of separation, and the conclusion of weeks spent in crossing the ocean and travelling by train inland. Anna too had been amazed at the size and grandeur of Canada. Its widely separated settlements, its great distances, its newness – everything was so different from England that at first it seemed frightening. But that feeling was now past. Today she would be with David again, would find out how things were with him, and get some inkling about their future. They had spent too much time apart; she needed him. Being at his side and working out their future was more important than any other consideration. She was certain of that.

The local train they had taken from Belleville seemed exasperatingly slow. She could even count the fence posts as they passed leisurely by. But the train was moving, and bringing her nearer to David; the station at Madoc had to appear eventually.

The children were no less impatient to see their father again. How pleasant it would be to get out into those great open spaces they could see and roam around exploring. The forests seemed endless. Almost wherever they looked there were trees and they could be frightening. What wild animals were hidden there, watching? Where were the Indians they had read about? Each of the older children had been delegated to look after certain pieces of luggage, and each was to check on the others to make doubly sure that no precious parcel or bag was left behind. Everyone had accepted his responsibilities seriously and seldom needed to be reminded of a duty. But, although they enjoyed the ever-changing scenery, all were eager for the journey to end.

David reached the station platform shortly before the train was due to pull in. His excitement at the coming meeting had kept mounting steadily. No longer could he stand or sit still, but paced back and forth beside the tracks, hands clasped behind him as he watched the curve in the distance whenever he faced in that direction, and unconsciously he hurried his pacing to turn that way again.

At last a wisp of smoke floating up over the far woods hinted the end to waiting. The sound of a whistle in the distance removed any doubt; the train was coming. As usual, a large group of spectators had gathered to watch this daily event. Every eye was focussed down the tracks.

The engine came in sight and crawled around the distant curve, pulling its chain of box-cars. Then the passenger coach near the end appeared, and the whole train straightened out as it approached the station. If Anna and the children were on board, it would end a long and lonely year of separation.

The engine swept past the platform in a hissing cloud of steam; the box-cars followed, thumping and clanking as the train slowed for the stop. Brake shoes gripped as the air was applied, showers of sparks flew out as they held the turning wheels. The brakeman on the coach steps signalled to the engineer, and with a final squeal and jerk the passenger car halted beside the watching crowd.

The conductor in his blue uniform swung down to the platform with the last motion of the coach. A trainman followed, carrying the stepping-box in one hand. He placed this at the foot of the car stairs and waited, ready to assist the passengers to alight. David worked his way through the crowd to be near enough to watch each person coming out of the door. First he saw Arthur and Eddie, each clutching a box or bundle. Florence and Katy followed, similarly loaded, and then he spied Anna with the new baby in her arms. David's eyes misted over with eagerness and joy, so that he did not even see Lily and Gertie emerge to make up the remainder of his group.

As each child stepped to the platform, it received his warm embrace, bundles and all. But it was for Anna that his strongest feelings were exposed. Bystanders mattered nothing as she stepped down and he gathered her in his arms. The lonely days of the long parting were over at last.

They all clung together, not wanting to be separated in these first moments of meeting. Bundles, packages, and boxes were set down against the station wall till each member could be admired and checked for a year's growth. The strangeness from long separation slowly melted away. Baby Johnnie in Gertie's arms became the centre of interest for a while as each had some detail to relate concerning him.

After a few more minutes, David and the boys loaded the luggage into the waggon that was waiting at the end of the platform where the horses were tied, soothed by a patient friend. It was now well on into the day, so that the long drive to Millbridge was out of the question till the morrow. David had engaged a room at a local boarding-house – all that was available since the next day marked the celebration of the twelfth of July, an event of great importance in Madoc at that time. The local Orange Lodge members walked in parade to celebrate the victory of the long-ago battle of the Boyne in Ireland, and lodges from neighbouring villages joined them. Accommodations were so limited that David had felt lucky at being able to obtain anything at all.

The family had the rest of the day to look around the town, do some necessary shopping, and rest from the long journey. Early in the morning they would set out for their drive to Millbridge, some twenty miles away.

Next morning, after a hearty breakfast, the Leveridges left Madoc behind. The sun had been up a short time and the air was warm and pleasant. A gentle breeze had risen; it would cool the heat of mid-day as well as carry away the clouds of dust that rose from the road as they drove along. The horses were fresh and knew that they were headed for home, so needed no urging to keep up a good pace whenever the state of the road made that possible.

Much of the roadway led through forests, which became more extensive the farther they went. Here and there, patches of land had been cleared in places where the hills were more gentle in height. Occasionally they passed a cheese factory, which had been built when a small settlement was able to support its operation. Small and less well-kept trails often led away from the main Hastings Road that they were following. Each of these led through the hills to a more remote settlement or village. Some of these distant places David had visited in his efforts to find work, and he was able to give a little information about them. He also knew the country crossroads stores that they passed on their way.

Eldorado was the name of one of the villages. David explained that it had been named for that fabulous but elusive gold mine after a small pocket of the precious metal had been discovered on a nearby farm. These small deposits of gold were quite commonly found in the area, but, to the disappointment of all, no mine yet found had proved extensive enough to support a continuous mining operation. Many of the settlers, however, were certain that one day an important discovery of a large and valuable deposit of minerals would be made somewhere in the county. This magnet drew venturesome people farther into the unknown and unsettled areas back in the woods. Anna could see that mining fever was taking hold of David's mind too and influencing his visions of the future.

Near Bannockburn they found an open spot where a stream crossed the road, and all were glad to stop for a bite to eat. The horses were unhitched and allowed to graze along the edge of the water and road while the family rested under the trees beside the way. But the period of rest was soon over and the drive resumed. The patches of clearing had grown steadily fewer, and

18

the wooded areas longer as the day passed. The hills seemed to be drawing closer together as well as rising higher. More rocky outcroppings were to be seen.

Towards the latter part of the afternoon, they passed the Millbridge country store, located at a crossroads. They turned off the main highway into a narrower and more woodsy way. Clearings had become restricted now to patches of land between the hills and rocks, although often a fairly level valley floor was to be seen where the neighbours were not so widely spaced.

Anna could not help but compare the road they were travelling on with those she had known in England. This one had grown progressively worse as the day advanced. Rocks were plentiful, especially in the middle of the track, away from where the wheels ground the surface finer and tended to pack it down more closely. Rains had washed away much of the finer gravel from the surface, leaving behind large stones that jolted their waggon.

This bouncing was much more noticeable where the way crossed a swamp or other low ground. To keep the wheels from sinking into the soft mud, tree trunks had been laid close together across the roadway and the whole foundation covered with gravel. But in many places the covering of gravel had been washed away by the rain, and the light waggon jolted severely as it crossed the bare logs. Such construction then was common in Canada. However, if the gravel were renewed often enough, it served very well and made a passable surface at a walking speed.

Anna had been watching the houses as well. The farther they travelled from the towns, the more humble the dwellings became. Most of them were built of logs, with few windows, and she judged that they must have low ceilings. Some did not even boast an upstairs and seemed too small to be divided into separate rooms. She wondered what her home would be like. David had said little about it, just that it was hard to find much of a house if one rented and wanted to be at all handy to where work was available.

Eventually they did draw up to such a house as she had been seeing. It appeared, from first glance, to have an upstairs area for there was a tiny window high up in the gable end. The cleared space around the building was quite small and the whole looked anything but prosperous.

Fortunately, Anna had a knack for making a house into a home. When their belongings had been carried indoors and David had driven away to return the borrowed waggon and team, she had time to look around more carefully and plan what to do. Each of the children was set to work and like magic the place's dreary look of desertion soon gave way to a fresher and homier appearance. At least, it was pleasant to know that their long journeying was over for a while. They would learn to practise the rugged pioneer prescription for getting ahead: make it do – use it up – do without.

Anna soon found that although her neighbours were widely scattered they welcomed her warmly into the community. At first their kindnesses and gifts embarrassed her because she could give nothing in return, although her skill at sewing made ample repayment possible later on.

But Anna spent many lonely hours, as she could not take all her children with her when she went visiting her new friends, nor could she leave them at home alone. David had returned to work. Now he must walk many miles after his day's work on

Saturday to spend a short time with his family, carrying with him most of the supplies they needed.

Building a short stretch at a time, the Rathbun Lumber Company was extending a railway north from Trenton through Hastings county to reach the pine forests. Each summer the line was pushed a little farther, giving access to new stands of timber for logging and bringing the outside world closer to the more remote settlements. Railway building and log cutting were heavy tasks. Long working days were expected of the men, but a job meant money coming in and brighter hopes for the future.

David wanted to own property. With so much vacant land all around him, surely he could find somewhere a suitable place for his family to settle and make a home. As yet he had not found what he wanted. It would have to be near some industry where he could get work when cash was needed. Nor was he ready to settle just anywhere. He felt confident that the time of fulfilment could not be far off, nor that magic place too distant. In the meantime, he would keep on working while he could.

Anna wrote frequently to her mother in England. Since postage at that time was expensive, many of her letters were "crossed" to save weight. That meant filling the sheet of paper in the ordinary way, then giving it a quarter-turn and writing the remainder of her message at right angles to and over what had been written already. This made the finished letter harder to read, but with Anna's clear and legible script it could be understood. Every penny spent had to be considered well before parting with it, even to pay for letters home.

Undoubtedly some of Anna's letters home were lost. But her mother saved many of them and later on they were returned to the family in Canada. They told about her life, with its hardships, its joys in simple things, and its abiding faith in the goodness of God. The following is one of the first letters she wrote after she arrived in Canada.

Millbridge / Sunday Morning

My dearest Mother, Father, and all

I was very glad indeed to get your letters and also Rosa's this week. I had been looking out for them. I don't know how long they had been lying at the Post Office, for as it is so far, we cannot go, and the neighbours bring each other's up, there is often someone going. I was glad to find you all well, as we are, thank God. The children look very well. Johnnie is got on very much, always out in the fresh air, and plenty of milk to drink. The children seem happy enough, and I am getting more used to the place now.

We are doing well at present. David took his first pay he had had since we came last night, over 50 dollars. He has now a great deal more owing him, as the system of payment is that when a man has worked two months he gets one month's pay; so he always has a month's pay owed him. He was agreeably surprised to find that the boys were going to get a dollar a day instead of 75 cents, so that they each earn 25s. a week. While we can do so, we shall keep here. Of course, it will be ended by and by, but there is always money to be earned all winter, as David was at work most of all last winter. The worst of it is that we are so far away from a church and school, shop and post office.

The man whose house this is keeps a shop, or store as they are called here, so David went up and paid his rent and some things we owed. He had 4 or 5 miles to go, after his work was done, and brought home some sugar and a pr of boots for Kate, a strong looking pr for a dollar, so I don't think they are so very dear. He did not get home till nearly 11. Arthur went with him. Edward came home to milk the cow. Some of the other men went up to be paid, so they were not alone all the way, but I should not have liked the walk.

Mr. Lumb, our landlord, wants me to go up as they have lately bought an organ. His daughters are learning to play. I shall go when I have a chance. I might often go out, but I don't care much about it as there is only Sunday when I can leave the children for long. This is a lonely place to leave them in alone, so I never go anywhere except down to Mrs. Pilgrim's. If I were to go there every day I should be welcome. She told me to give her kind remembrance to you, Mother, though she was a stranger to you and likely to be in this world. She hoped you and she would meet in a better.

I hope you have got my last letter I wrote, but I have to get people to take them, so they may sometimes be lost. I hope that you will all write pretty often and tell me all the news as this is so lonely. I read your letters over and over. Tell Father to give them all a good smoke, as, as soon as we opened the last one, we smelt Father's pipe and passed it around so we all had a whiff. Many thanks also for the newspaper, David and I were very glad of it. Send one when you can. Rosa talks of sending some. I was wishing someone who could afford it would take a cheap periodical such as the Quiver weekly and send it to us, as I miss the reading so much. I wish I had brought some books.

Give my love to Mr. and Mrs. Wright and to all inquiring friends. I don't feel as far away as I really am, as when we were on the voyage the motion is so gentle except when we were inside and still, that we could scarcely realize we were going. When we were in mid ocean for a few days the ship pitched from one side to the other, [so] that sometimes when you wanted to go to one place you found yourself against your will running to another, which caused many a laugh. One of these times I think about writing an account of it all more in detail, if you would care for me to do so. I like London; not at all like Norwich.

I don't think that I will write any more now as it is almost bed time here, getting early morning with you. I must conclude now, with love from the children and David and myself to you all.

> I remain your loving and affectionate Anna
> God Bless you all

Besides her frequent letters to her Mother, Anna wrote to her sisters and occasionally to other members of the family at home in England. Some of these letters were passed along to her mother for keeping and to be read again and again, as Anna had mentioned doing herself with those she received.

Anna's sisters, Rosa, Fannie, Gertie, and Mary, were mentioned with considerable frequency during the period that these letters cover. Anna always hoped that others of her family would come out to Canada to settle down. She knew that this would be the only way she ever would see any of her relatives again. She and David never would be wealthy enough to go to England for a visit. Their large family would take all that they earned, and by the time all her family had grown up enough to look after themselves her parents would not be living. Two of her sisters, Mary and Gertie, did eventually come to Canada, where they married and settled down. But they both lived in towns where life was a little easier than homesteading in the backwoods.

As the summer in Millbridge passed and autumn began to colour the scenery, David heard more and more often tales about a small settlement in the woods forty miles north. These stories told of a new mining development at Coe Hill, where iron ore had been found in what seemed to be commercial quantities. It looked as though this could grow into an important industry. The railroad was going to be extended to reach Coe Hill the following summer. So David planned on going to see the place for himself in the hope it might be what they looked for. But again, as in England, he said nothing to his family of his plans, as there was a chance that they might amount to nothing. He decided that he would walk to Coe Hill during the late fall weather when his job ended.

David had discovered that he really liked to walk. The lure of unknown places was strong in his mind. He enjoyed seeing a new view from the top of each new hill, and finding out what lay around the next bend in the road. He had had to walk much since coming to Canada and he felt that as a result he lived closer to the earth. A day and a half each way would suffice for the journey unless the road was entirely too bad to be followed easily.

As the summer days began to shorten noticeably and unmistakable signs of fall appeared, Anna began to think more often of the coming winter. The neighbours told tall tales of what she could expect; David said little, outside of admitting that there was plenty of snow and that some days were cold. Anna could not help but wonder what lay ahead. A letter to her sister was different from one to her mother, even though she knew that all letters were passed from hand to hand at home.

Millbridge / Nr Madoc / Hastings Co. / Ontario / Canada

My dearest Gertie,

I was very glad to get a letter from you at last, and to hear that you are so well and happy at Clare. No doubt the near presence of Mr. (what's his name) makes it seem so delightful. I know how it was when I went a courting. You must tell me all about him and describe his personal appearance when you write again. I confess to being very partial to young men myself, always was. I remember your writing to me at Hochering and saying that you had got a young man, your 49th flame. Is this one the same? Or is he No. 50?

I wonder what you would think of this dull spot; you thought the Park Farm dull. Here, if we see a man at a distance, we all run out and watch him as if he were a rarity, and the children say, "Oh, there's a man."

The air is very pure here, and we get it fresh and strong; it is reckoned a healthy place. The children all look remarkably well. I don't know how we shall like the winter. Mr. Shearing told me the air was very clear and the sun bright most of the time. They have heavy snowstorms, of course. People say last winter was the sharpest known for 40 years, so perhaps it won't be so bad this time.

Was it not strange that David and I met again the same day twelve months that he went away? He left Hochering July 11th, 1882; and we met at Madoc on July 11th, 1883. I meant to have mentioned it before, but it slipped my mind.

I must make haste and finish this, for the girls are going down to Mr. Pilgrim's to ask him to take it when he goes to the Jordan tomorrow. You say in your letter that one here need not dress much. Not here, perhaps, but in the towns they are very smart and dress in the height of fashion. Fashions here seem to be similar to English ones.

The farmers here make a great deal of the material they use. They spin their own wool, also they make their own sugar, [and] kill their own meat; so they are very independent.

We should go to see Mrs. Peacock on Sunday. She has asked me so many times that I feel quite ashamed, and they are busy every day but Sunday. She is expecting another increase. I asked her how she did, as there is no doctor nearer than Madoc, a distance of over 20 miles. She said she has never had a doctor. They get a woman who is good at such times and do the best they can. She says you must make up your mind that if you are to live, you'll live; and if you die, you die: a comfortable sort of feeling.

Hoping to hear from you again soon, and to have a nice long letter. With love from all to you.

I remain
Yr loving sister
Anna

7

Late fall brought the closing up of jobs for David and his boys. No more steady work could be expected till the logging camps opened after winter had set in. Early one morning in November, therefore, David told Anna that he was going to look for work and might be gone upwards of a week. He decided that now was the time to go to see whether the Coe Hill iron mine was a real possibility, or just a false alarm as so many other mines had turned out to be.

Most of the leaves had fallen now, letting the sunlight penetrate deeper into the forests that the road wound through as David swung along the Hastings Road at a good pace, travelling lightly through the leaves rustling underfoot. Not far out of Millbridge he came to a hill well known as "The Hole in the Wall." When he crossed the stream at its foot and started up the slope, it didn't appear worthy of its reputation, but as he rounded one hairpin turn after another it became steeper and steeper. When he did reach the top, he was quite ready to rest and agree that the name was aptly chosen.

Later in the day he climbed another hill of almost equal height, but here the road ran straight up a more gradual slope. The road-makers had named the knoll Pine Hill, since the road cut through a majestic grove of those trees so much in demand for their lumber.

The mastering of these two hills brought David up on to a plateau where the land levelled out gradually and the going became easier. There were few homesteads along the way. When he did come to one, he was as glad to stop for a chat as the owners were pleased to see him come along and give them an excuse for quitting their work for a few minutes. In one such place he accepted the pressing offer of a night's lodging and joined the family for supper and breakfast.

Late on the following morning he crossed a small river that wound its way across a flat area in the midst of a heavy pine forest. From there he walked up a slope to Coe Hill, named after the two discoverers of the mine.

A few houses near a combined store and post office, a busy blacksmith shop, a boarding-house, and a couple of mine buildings in the distance made up the community. But the place had an air of permanence that pleased David as soon as he saw it. Anyone to whom he talked glowed about the prospects of a bright future for the settlement. David wanted to believe these tales and hoped that his long search for a home was over.

But first he had to find somewhere for his family to live. Here he met difficulty. The story was the same as in other new areas – there were no unoccupied houses. David began to inquire for land that he could buy or homestead. He wanted a place where the land was good, that was not too far out of the way, and where there would be a neighbour handy.

Fortunately he met someone who had just what was required. This man had filed a claim on a hundred acres of good bush and started a clearing near a friend who had settled there previously. But now the man decided that pioneering was not for him, and was ready to sell. So he and David walked five miles north and looked at the lot. The sale was made, and a part of the purchase price paid.

Thus it was with elation that David set out to rejoin his family at Millbridge. Now he could tell them about the new prospects. Then he would return shortly, and with the help of his new neighbour and other settlers, would build a shanty to shelter Anna and the children until he could afford to provide them with something better.

During November, the daylight hours shortened quickly, noticeable particularly on cloudy days when the pattern of fall weather changed to the steadier cold of the winter season. But a few days of soft and lovely warmth came along as a teaser. Although the family knew it could be only a temporary pause, all enjoyed soaking up the warmth from the gentle flow of mildness from the south.

But the respite soon passed. One morning the sun rose in a flaming red sky, the heavens blazing as long streamers of high clouds glowed in the morning light. Older and weatherwise men watched and shook their heads, knowing that Indian summer was on its way out. The air was almost entirely still. This peacefulness lasted till close to sundown, when gentle fingers of breeze stroked down from the north. The sun set behind a bank of clouds that thickened through the evening. The breeze increased to become a wind that grew ever colder, searching out cracks and other openings in walls and roofs to suck away the heat from indoors.

During the night, the gale howled and whistled around the corners of the house, carrying with it the first flakes of a snowstorm. People crawled shivering from their beds in the morning to build up the fire, attempting to counteract the grimness of the hissing snowflakes driven against the frosted-over panes of glass in the windows. It was a day to stay indoors when possible and keep the fire burning steadily.

Cracks around windows were stuffed with rags to keep the cold out and the heat in. Doors, shrinking with the frost, opened up new cracks that were hastily stopped up. A rug was rolled and laid against the doorway to block the narrow space underneath and keep the snow and the draft out. Each time the door was opened, someone inside hastily pushed back this rug to its former position. Without it, the floor soon became icy cold. The chair behind the stove became the favourite spot for cosiness.

In every home, people made the accustomed preparations for the winter's extremes of cold. Anna and her family tried to adapt themselves to this new experience. After the first few days they had organized a pattern of living to combat the cold. But winter also brought delights: the brightness of clear days, sparkling crisp snow and air, rosy cheeks tingling with cold, and the thrill of proving themselves able to meet the new challenge.

Whispers of this new pleasure crept into Anna's letters home.

Millbridge / Nr Madoc / Hastings Co. / Ontario / Canada/Sunday Aft

My dearest Fanny

I was exceedingly glad to get another letter from you this last week and hope you have received one from me by this time. I also had one from Rosa at the same time, which I must answer. I count very much of getting your letters, but one thing I must mention now I think of. Send thin paper if possible as if it is the least trifle over weight they charge 10¢ (5.) for it. I have had to pay twice, which makes the letters come dear; excuse my mentioning the same.

I was glad to find you all as usual, as we are, thank God, and going on much the same. Edward's work is finished and Arthur's nearly so. David's also will not last much longer, so we will soon have much less coming in, and our future course is uncertain. David thinks after this work is done of going himself farther back to see if there is work at an iron mine; and if there is and he can get a house, we shall move up. But while there is work to be had, he does not like to leave it. We may stay here the winter and live on what money we have with what work he can get while the weather is open. It is a good thing we are placed so that he will not be forced to go out when the weather is very bad.

I don't know what sort of winter this is going to be, but it is very cold now at times; sharp frosts, ice indoors in our back place which is very open. We have moved our beds downstairs now and made ourselves as comfortable as circumstances will admit, as it was too exposed upstairs. So we sleep and live all in one room. It is a very large one, so there is plenty of room; it is more comfortable.

We have bought a nice looking bedstead and 6 chairs, and David nailed some boards over the stump of a table that was here, so it does for a makeshift. We have our stove in the middle and can keep up as warm a fire as we like, getting all firing for the trouble of getting it ready. Edward is getting a good axe-man and keeps me pretty well supplied. A piece or two of wood in the stove casts as much heat in the room as a large fire in our English ones. When I have a fire large enough to bake with, we can hardly bear ourselves near it.

I have made some very good butter lately and a nice new cheese, so you see I am getting quite a dairy woman. I like the work very well. We like my butter better than what I have been buying. Our old cow goes on very well. We still keep the one of Mr. Russell's which we hired. He came to take it home the other day, but she would not go, gave him a pretty chase, so he said we might keep her as long as we liked for nothing. I have been doing a few odd jobs of sewing for him, as he lives all alone, doing everything that is done himself.

Mrs. Pilgrim went to Madoc, so she laid out some money for me as well as for herself. I don't know how I should have got groceries or other things if it had not been for her. As she says, she does for me the same as if I were her own child. She bought me two prs of dark blankets, 2 dollars and $\frac{1}{2}$ a pr, which is dear, is it not? 1£ for 4 blankets. Woolen things are dearer here. Then she got me some flannel for the boys [for] some warm winter shirts, and some linsey or wincey for a frock for the girls. So I have plenty of sewing in hand. Then I have ordered some full-cloth, as the homemade cloth is called here, for warm trousers for the boys. They have earned them.

I am getting more used to this place now and don't feel so strange as I did at first. If we continue to get on, and were within walking distance of a church and school, I should like it much better. Our neighbours don't like the idea of our leaving here and suggest all sorts of plans to keep us here.

Mr. Pilgrim brought us a letter for Arthur from his Cousin Arthur, and one from Polly for Florence. They were finely pleased and will answer them before long. He also brought us a paper from you, for which please accept our thanks; and some British Workwoman from Harleston, I think, which we were finely glad of. Anything of that sort is acceptable. I should think that Aunt might send us some. I thought cousin Bessie would have sent us a letter before this. We were sorry to hear of Mr. Lowell's death, I forget what he ailed. The children were very pleased with Ernest's and Freddy's letters.

We are pleased to hear you have so many apples. They are very scarce and dear in the backwoods here. Out more in the west they are grown more, some places very plentiful. Is Rachel thinking of coming to America? Give my love to them all. Did Anna Child ever come out? It is a good job you are such a favorite with Robert's wife, especially if she has many such parcels as the one you mentioned. She is like the rest of us, I suppose, she will not let the name die down. I am sorry Miss Brown still holds so badly, give my best respects to her. I suppose you send the letters to Mother when you get one.

I am glad to find the harvest is plentiful in England. We don't know much about the harvest here, as there is not much corn cultivated about. The land is wonderfully rocky on the surface, and under the ground the stones and rocks lie everywhere. Mr. Pilgrim had a little wheat.

Now I must conclude this and write a letter to Rosa, so I will say Good-bye and God Bless you. I often wish you were here to have a chat with when I sit down to sew. With love and kisses to all, I remain

Yr loving sister Anna

Write again soon

Millbridge/Hastings Co./Ontario/Canada/Nov. 12th [1883]

My dearest Mother and all

I was very glad to get your letter yesterday, as I had not had one for some time. I suppose you write when you hear from me, and I write when I hear from you; you must not be alarmed or think anything is the matter if you do not hear from me when you expect, as I have often a letter written a week or two before I can get it posted.

I am sorry to find you still suffer so much with your old complaint; you must take care of yourself and not think you are no use. You seem to me, and always did, as if you were the hand that bound us all together; and whether the seas divide us or not, there is the same feeling, for it is a heart feeling that I believe we all experience.

I was glad to hear the rest all as usual, and thank you for your kind letters, and also for the "Sunday at Home," of which I have received two. I have not had time to read them to-day as we have been to Mr. Pilgrim's to dinner. She sends her Christian love to you all. I went down two days last week and took my machine and did her a good bit of sewing, which she was glad of and would have paid me for, but after her kindness to me I was glad to do her something in return.

We are all well, I am glad to say. David and the boys are out of work now. David has been trying and walking miles, last week more than eighty miles, to try to get a house near some work going on, but has not succeeded yet. There is plenty of work going on, but in out of the way places where there are no houses. They build up a house for the men to lodge and board in. I am afraid I shall have to make up my mind to be left alone a good bit this winter, as if he gets work he will be too far to come home at night. I should not mind it if I were in a village or near some other houses, but it will be very lonely for me in the winter time too.

We have had fine open weather at present, one shower of snow that was soon gone. To-day was lovely. I saw a butterfly out, and on the 5th of Nov we saw several. Still they say we may expect the snow down any day now, and when it comes it does not go away till May. So that is something to look forward to.

No work goes on particularly, only what is necessary. The farmers discharge their labourers, if they keep any (and I don't know any that do about here). They only employ them [at] the busiest time and work them from sunrise to sunset. So I consider the labourers about here are no better, if as well off, as they are in England. The railways are good, but they are very slow of payment. They owe us 150 dollars. We shall not get it all at once either. We expect to take some next week. We have to pay well for anything being done here. We had some flour come in; we had to pay a dollar for bringing it in only 5 miles. So money soon goes. We don't see such a thing as an apple here. I miss them very much. And potatoes are dear, we paid 50 cents a bushel for some and not good at that. Meat is cheap, 7 cents a lb [for] mutton.

I hope you will send foreign paper, as I nearly always have to pay 10 cents for your letters. We had a paper from Mrs. Anderson and one from Fanny. I had also a nice letter from Cousin Bessie, which I will answer soon. Thank you for your good wishes on my birthday. I made the children, big and little, some good toffee. We don't get any fish [in] these parts, but they are plentiful in some places. We may go that way some day. As for beer, I have never seen any since I have been in the country. It is sold at the villages and towns, but whiskey is the drink of the country, and the curse of it too. Many men work hard and earn a deal of money and then spend it in whiskey and nearly kill themselves.

I wish you could knit me a counterpane. Wool is so dear here, stocking wool 75 cents a lb, and flannel as dear. Grey calico is dear too. I made some for Mrs. Pilgrim, 12 cents a yd, which we could have got in England for $2\frac{1}{2}$ or 3.

34

This is a stormy night. The wind howls around the house. I expect winter will soon set in. If we stay here, David is going to plaster the house up to keep the cold out. The boys were pleased with your letter and will write before long. They are good, handy boys and do a good deal. They have kept me in firewood at present, but their Father will have to get some piled if he goes out. I was very pleased with Father's nice long letter. Give my kind love to Mary and him and thank them both, they must take this as an answer.

I must finish this letter in a hurry this morning as David is going up to the Jordan where the post office is. It is very cold this morning, quite a change from yesterday, so I suppose winter is coming in earnest.

Now I must conclude with kind love and kisses to all friends and all at home. I will write again soon, and write to me as soon as you can, as having letters is the principal event of my life just now. Love from David and all the children, in which I join. Today last year in Hochering I was confined, the time has passed away since then. I wonder what the next year will bring forth. Give my love to Gertie and wish her many happy returns on her birthday. The last one she spent in Hochering. Goodbye once again. God bless you all.

Anna

After the cold weather came in earnest, it was quite evident to David and Anna that the house could not be used in the same way during the severe cold of a Canadian winter as in the warmth of summer. They drew in closer to the centre of the building, leaving first the shell of a summer kitchen built on to the back. Then, when the nights grew still colder, they abandoned the upstairs, which had become little warmer than the out-of-doors. The whole family grouped in the one downstairs room.

The stove was placed in the middle of the floor, and during the day radiated warmth in every direction. But at night the fire burned low and the cold strengthened, letting the frost creep indoors; often the water pail standing on a shelf close to the door froze over. On the colder nights David tried to rouse himself several times to replenish the fire, but not always did he catch the bed of coals in time to produce a flame on the new supply of wood he added.

There was no work available in the neighbourhood for himself or for the boys. They busied themselves in cutting the wood needed for the stove, and, on many mornings, shovelling away snow from the paths leading to the woodpile, outbuildings, and well.

The little shanty on his Coe Hill property was often in David's thoughts. Since it was a new building it should be reasonably weather tight, even though it had been put up hastily and with green logs. He had learned much about building from the men who had helped with its forming, following the pioneer methods of construction. One of the last things they had done to prepare the shanty was to move in and set up a stove that David bought second-hand from another settler.

Were they all living there now, these tedious days doing little of real value could be spent in chopping out the many trees on the piece of ground which he thought would make a good garden. He remembered well the small clearing that was already chopped. If it were burned early in the spring, it could be cultivated in time to plant potatoes or a little wheat, to provide some of their food for the following winter.

A chat that David had had with a young neighbour at Coe Hill (anyone living within three or four miles was a neighbour) came to mind. This man suggested:

"You should move in on your place in the winter. The swamps are frozen then. The snow fills up the worst places on the roads. Travelling by sleigh is easier than using a waggon later on. Then you're Johnny-on-the-spot to chop your new clearing or start your spring work without losing the time it takes to move in."

When David hesitated about bringing young children into a cold house in the middle of the winter, Mr. Hewton replied:

"Come and stay with us for a few days till you get things ready and the house warmed up. It's only a couple of miles from your place by road, hardly a mile across the woods. That's about next door. Our house is small, but there'd be room. We'd just squeeze a little closer together for a while."

This generous offer David accepted. He had hoped that maybe the Elliotts, living in actual sight of his shanty, might have made a similar offer; but they had a houseful of their own family, some of whom were elderly. They had been most helpful in giving skilled aid towards putting up the cabin, and David was truly grateful for that. He already loved that tiny, one-roomed building nestled in his woods; much of himself had gone into its making – the first home he had ever owned.

He and Anna had saved some money from the work during the fall. Soon he would collect the last owing him and could leave. Anna would like to spend Christmas among the new friends that she always was quick to make. When David's plan was clear he discussed the situation with her. She did not object, what David had planned for them was what she wanted too. Anna had known that he was not happy where they were living. She knew that he longed to be on a place of their own, as she herself did. If they were going to leave, and they certainly would have to, then the sooner they did so, the better for all concerned.

No one in Millbridge wished to see David and Anna go, and many hopes were expressed that the trip would be easy. It was sure to be cold, and the distance meant they must stop overnight at some point in the journey. Anna's story of the moving follows, but only a part of this letter remains.

Faraday Post Office / Faraday / Hastings Co / Ontario / Canada

My dearest Mother and all,

I dare say you will have wondered at my silence, but I have had a muddling time and I thought that I would not write till I was settled. Again, you will see by the heading of this letter that we are away from Millbridge. We are got to Wollaston, 28 or 30 miles from there. David has bought a hundred acres of land and built a shanty on it, in which we have just come to live. It is not all paid for yet, of course. It belonged to a young man who did not care to live on it. He charged 100 dollars, 50 of which is paid. Also there will have to be either 50 or 100 dollars paid to government, 20 of which is paid. The other is due in yearly instalments.

The shanty cost quite a bit to build, about 40 dollars, and it cost us quite a bit to move up here, so that we are got pretty bare again. David will have to go to work away from home about 5 miles, so he will have to board out. We wanted to have had enough money to live on for a year so that he could have been at home and worked on the land. Still as it is we must make the best of it and be very careful for a time. One thing, we shall have no rent to pay, and heaps of firewood, which is a good thing.

There is 4 or 5 acres chopped, and everyone says the land is good. So I hope, please God, we shall get a living, if it is a rough one. I like this much better than at Millbridge, for I have a neighbour near. I can see their shanty from ours, and they are within

call. They have been very kind to David while he was backwards and forwards here, and I think I shall like them for neighbours.

The woods here are not so dense as at Millbridge, but the land is wonderfully hilly. It is two miles off the road here, and it seems like climbing up a mountain. There are not many wolves about here also, but more bears. Mr. Elliott, my neighbour, has killed six since he has been here, and 15 deer this fall, as autumn is called here. I have had some venison several times. It is very nice. They say that bears are afraid of people and always run away.

Our shanty is a strange place, just a one roomed house, made entirely of trunks of trees, 12 ft. by 20, the trees just as they are felled, with the bark on. It is put up without nails or anything of the kind. The corners are hewed so that they fit one into another, mortised, I think it is called. The roof is made of basswood logs hewed into troughs; the first lot laid with the bark inside and the hollow parts outside. Then over these, where the two troughs meet, other troughs are laid with the bark uppermost, so that the water cannot run through.

The floor is lumber, as boards are called here; two little windows, one at each end, and a door in the side facing south. That, dear Mother, is my present home. I have been busy to-day putting things as straight as I can; and David has been putting some shelves up.

I was wondering to-day what you would think of it. How different everything is from my past life. There is a pretty view in front, a wooden hill partially cleared. When summer comes, I shall be going up to see what is beyond it, but now the snow is a foot and $\frac{1}{2}$ thick on the level, so we can't go far. There is a road through the woods, but it is like climbing up little mountains and going down again.

You will want to know all about our journey. It was quite an undertaking this time of the year with all the little children, but, thank God, we are got here all right. It is awfully cold; and the shanty, being new and green, is not as warm as it will be. We are obliged to keep good fires, but firing is cheap, and it lies around the house.

We left Millbridge on the Thursday after Christmas, started with part of our things, the beds and stove, etc., about 8 in the morning. We were packed in a sleigh, which is like a long wooden box set on runners instead of wheels, the horses with bells. We glided over the snow, up hill and down dale, sometimes nearly out on one side, sometimes nearly out on the other. I had to put all the children's warm clothing on and wrap blankets round them, but it was not as sharp then as it is now.

When we were got a short distance away from home, nearly up to Mr. Russell's, the sleigh broke down. One of the runners broke. So out we all had to get, and tramp through the snow to Mr. Russell's, while the young man went five miles back to fetch another sleigh. I was thankful it did not happen when we were out on the road away from any habitation, we must have perished of cold; it delayed us three hours, so we did not get to our journey's end that day but had to take lodgings.

The people treated us kindly, and I might have got rid of Gertie there [they seemed to like her so much]. Next morning we started off again. It was bitterly cold. I had all I could do to keep myself and the children warm. Awful hilly roads; one hill was so steep we had to get out and walk. Sometimes the horses came down the hills sliding. I felt very frightened, but we got safely to our destination, which was at the home of a Mr. Hewton, who offered to take us in for 2 or 3 days till our place was aired out.

So we took them by storm, myself and seven children, 1 dog and 1 cat, besides beds and bedclothes. They are young people. She put me in the mind of sister Gertie. She is only 20, and was married when she was 16, 2 little children. We stayed there a week, only one room to live in. I shall be a long time getting used to such ways; however, I was forced to put the best face I could on the matter. They did not mind it.

When David and the young man got down to the shanty, they found the stove broken all to pieces. So David had to go back again and buy ... [letter ends here].

9

At first, the shanty home seemed strange because so many people had to live so close together, but, as the days went by, the family grew accustomed to the confined quarters. The small variety of food available gave sameness to all their meals and they were not always too well filled, even though their hearty appetites cleaned up every scrap of food put before them.

The highlight of the week was when David walked the five miles home from his work to spend Sunday with his family. The boys went part way to meet him and helped carry the bag of flour or other parcels of food that he brought each time. Occasionally, as well as the necessities, there was a small treat for everyone.

During the week, the boys could go out to chop and enlarge the clearing, which got them out of the crowded house for part of the time; they enjoyed that work. The hardest problem was finding something worth while for the older girls to do, but quite soon an answer came to that problem. Mrs. Hewton asked whether it might be possible for Gertie to come and stay with her family and help with the children. No money would be paid, but her living would be provided as well as sometimes a little new clothing.

The Hewtons had become good friends immediately; this offer pleased everyone and made Gertie's days more satisfying. Anna was sorry to have her family begin to break up, but Gertie's absence did help by giving more room at home and fewer to feed.

Soon another neighbour asked to have Florence come to live with her on the same basis. The two girls were in neighbouring homes and could visit each other easily. Anna was left with the two younger girls, Katy and Lily, at home. Baby Johnnie was everyone's pet and kept the family interested in his training.

The high hills near the new home had seemed massive and grim to Anna at first. But it wasn't long before she and David learned to accept and then even like them. They found strength in their ruggedness, shelter in their protection from the strong winds and storms, and challenge in learning to master them.

Finally, Anna came to love the heights that encircled her shanty home. Their firmness and strength comforted her lonely hours, gave a quietness and serenity that supported her through difficult times, and provided a feeling of safety that she had not known before. Like the Psalmist, she could lift up her eyes unto the hills around and feel freshness of faith coming from their presence. Daily family worship strengthened this feeling.

The woods, too, had been frightening to her. But this fear changed to wonder and delight when spring laid a carpet of wild flowers on the forest floor and birds sang everywhere. The trees, too, became friendly and sheltering, ready to reveal their secrets to anyone who wished to learn about them.

As the weeks passed and the family became better acquainted with the people in the area, the neighbourhood seemed to grow more like home. The Leveridges at first were more friendly with the families living towards the west and a little north. This settlement was known as Faraday, drawing its name from the township in which it was located.

The Faraday post office was located in one of the homes. A small Anglican church had been built in the settlement shortly before David and Anna came, and this was a big inducement for them to visit regularly. A walk to service on a Sunday morning always included calling at the post office for the chance of getting mail from home. Thus Faraday became the first focus of their interest.

The family continued to worship with the congregation of the Faraday church for several years. Sunday was the day for visiting to see how all the neighbours were getting along, a day of rest from ordinary work, and for keeping in touch with other families. Everyone gathered at church, listened to the sermon, and then spent the rest of the day renewing friendships and discussing common problems.

David continued to work in Coe Hill while there was a job to be had there. All mail came first to Coe Hill and then was despatched to several points from that centre, so it was natural that eventually the family was attracted more and more towards going to Coe Hill for most of their needs, including their mail.

After the completion of the railroad into the community, the Coe Hill mine developed quickly and flourished for a time. Shafts were dug, ore was raised and dumped to form a rusty pile at the end of the railroad where it was loaded on railway cars and sent out to Trenton to be treated. Then came a rumour that a smelter might be built in Coe Hill. If that should happen, a prosperous and swiftly growing town would develop quickly.

Time passed and spring came. Its arrival broke the greatest isolation that Anna had known in all her life. The fact that she and her family had survived that time of testing became a peg to secure her faith in the future, like pegs driven into the joints of a new building to hold the members together. Anna's next letter to her mother expresses some of her concern at being in such an out-of-the-way corner of the woods. But she did not yield to despair. Seldom did she complain to her mother about the new surroundings. This letter is incomplete, but enough remains to show Anna's depth of feeling as well as the loneliness of her existence in the shanty home.

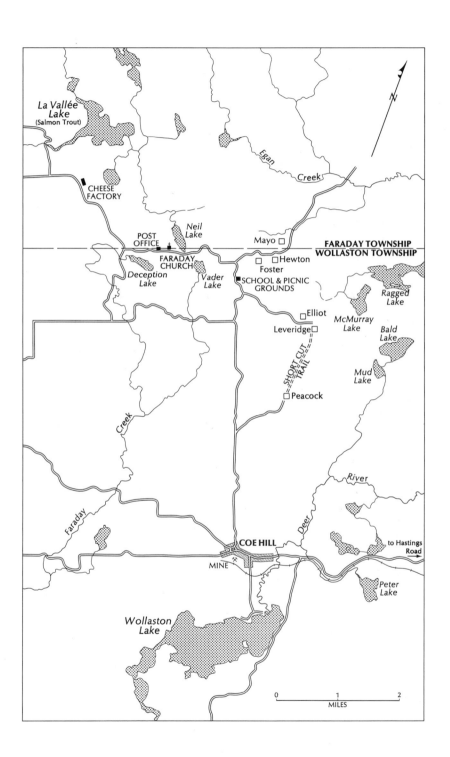

La Vallée Lake
(Salmon Trout)

CHEESE
FACTORY

Egan   Creek

Neil
Lake

POST
OFFICE

Mayo □

FARADAY TOWNSHIP
WOLLASTON TOWNSHIP

FARADAY
CHURCH

□ □*Hewton*
Foster

Deception
Lake

Vader
Lake

■SCHOOL & PICNIC
GROUNDS

Ragged
Lake

□*Elliot*

McMurray
Lake

Bald
Lake

Leveridge□

Mud
Lake

SHORT CUT
TRAIL

□*Peacock*

River

Creek

Deer

Faraday

COE HILL

to Hastings
Road

MINE

Peter
Lake

Wollaston
Lake

0   1   2
MILES

Faraday P.O. / Faraday / Hastings Co / Ontario / Canada

My dearest Mother and all:

I thought tonight I would commence a letter to you, though I don't know when you will get it as I have to get neighbours to take it to the post office, and then it lies there a week before it is sent to Madoc, which is our nearest town 60 miles off.

We are 30 miles further in the backwoods than we were before; 60 miles from a doctor, but I daresay in the course of time this will be a more thickly populated place and have institutions of its own. In the meantime, we that are used to different things, find ourselves badly off. When David cannot get a neighbour to bring it for him, he will have to carry all our flour 5 miles on his back. We are 5 miles from the store, and the snow very deep; but the winter is wearing away, thank God, and everything will be alive again.

David is still at work on the railway, but wages are only a dollar a day, and some days they can't work. It costs him 3 dollars out of that for his board and lodging. He may be able, when the spring opens, to get work so he can board at home, which I shall be thankful for, for those boarding houses are not very choice. Some of the lodgers are dirty and he brings home in his clothes now and then what I could well dispense with; but what can't be cured must be endured.

I should feel lonely indeed if it were not for my neighbours. I like to sit at my window and see them about their place. They are going to build themselves a house in the summer. They have been drawing the logs out of the forest ready. There is always something going on there, people in and out. I go in now and then and get a good dinner or tea, which is all the same, for they eat meat and potatoes three times a day.

They killed three fat pigs a little time ago. That is how they do about here. Then they pack it in salt in large barrels and it lasts them till they hunt the deer. Then they live on them. I tried to get some meat of them, but they will not part with any, so we have to live as we can. [We] don't get very fat. I hope if we do well we shall have some pigs of our own one day. I wish we had a little money to start with, as it will be some time before we can see much from the land, and David working out all the time.

You will be surprised to hear Florence and Gertie are both away from home. Mrs. Hewton, where we stayed the week we came here, took a fancy to Gertie and begged me to let her stay the rest of the winter with her as she is so lonely when her husband is out; and a few days ago the young farmer from the next farm to Mr. Hewton and quite near his, came over and asked me to spare Florence for company for his wife, and to rock the cradle. There is ... [letter ends here].

Spring, long awaited, came haltingly. Much work was needed to prepare the ground for planting a garden. As the snow disappeared, sticks, branches, and chips large and small appeared all over the clearing. Some undergrowth remained from the chopping and stumps were everywhere. Smaller ones were uprooted and dug out, but the larger stayed and Anna planted the garden around them.

The job of cleaning up began as soon as possible. Everyone helped. The younger children gathered up the chips and piled them against the shanty wall to dry for quick summer fires in the stove. They collected the smaller branches into big piles to burn after the sun had dried them out. As each spot was cleared and the frost came out of the ground, the boys dug it up. They turned under the old leaves, tore out masses of roots, and loosened up the new, black soil. Each day a little more ground was ready for planting.

When the plots were prepared, Anna did the seeding. Those vegetables that didn't suffer from chilly nights were planted before the more tender ones. Katy and Lily loved to work in the garden, and even did some of the lighter work of loosening up the soil. Johnnie, too, was ready to help, but needed watching and guidance.

Anna saw that each child had a place for making his own personal garden of vegetables or flowers. The main area was planted so as to use all space to the best advantage and provide a good supply of food for the next winter, and everyone was expected to do his share in the big garden before tending his private plot. Thus early in life Anna's children learned the pleasure of getting the soil ready, planting the seeds, and tending garden plots; they experienced the satisfaction of seeing the first shoots appear, develop into sturdy plants, and mature into flowers, fruits, or vegetables.

The soil was rich, dark, and loamy from centuries of rotting leaves on the floor of the forest, but it was hard work preparing the ground for the first garden and then keeping it clean. Other plants wanted to grow in that open, sunny space. Enormous ferns shot up from heavy underground roots which had not been completely removed. Young tree growth emerged everywhere as the forest tried to renew itself. Sucker shoots grew from some of the stumps, fed by the remaining root systems, and had to be cut away. Always there was much to do, but willing hands looked after that precious garden, their first in the new land.

Soon the whole family was intensely proud of the results. Fed by the richness of the new soil and watered by frequent spring showers, the garden grew splendidly. When there had been no rain for a week or more, the children carried pails of water from a creek flowing by near the edge of the garden. Like other things that are loved and get the attention they crave, everything Anna and her children planted thrived luxuriantly through the first few years in the new home.

Even Johnnie's little garden flourished, although his methods were not always the best. One day his mother found him pulling up beans and dipping their heads into a pail of water to give them a drink.

The coming of spring released Anna from the imprisoned feeling that winter had brought. There was a new freedom of movement around the area, and more opportunity for meeting neighbours. It was pleasant to laugh with them, discuss problems, help or give comfort when needed. Life seemed to speed up as the days warmed. Getting out of doors was a real pleasure; spring gave a lift to their spirits, brought zest to living.

A few sunny, peaceful days passed in ideal weather before the tormentors came. Soon after these balmy days hordes and myriads of mosquitoes plagued the family viciously by day at their work and by night in the cabin. A short while later, these fiends were supplemented by tiny black flies that added misery to daylight hours. They gave no warning hum as did the mosquitoes, but crawled into clothing and around the head at the hair-line. There they fed, drawing blood and leaving a mass of scabs when their bites sealed over.

These pests made life miserable during June and into July, when at last they faded away, having lived for their season. The only relief came from a smudge-pot, for its fumes drove the insects back. A few chips smouldering in the bottom of a pail with leaves or green grass piled on top produced a heavy, thick smoke. This brought some relief around the shanty on calm days. When there was a breeze outdoors, it blew most of the insects back into the shelter of the forest.

Anna's next letter speaks of some of her pleasure from meeting and mingling with her neighbours.

Faraday P.O. / Faraday / Hastings Co / Ontario / Canada

My dearest Mother, Father, and all:

I was very glad to get your letter this week, also dear Mary's. I was looking out for one, and I am glad you are all as usual. We are all quite well, thank God. I fancy our letters must nearly always cross each other, as no doubt you have had another from me more lately, for I always write soon after the receipt of yours. I guess you feel the coldness of the spring very much, and it must greatly affect your rheumatics.

We are having just such changeable weather; a few weeks ago we had it so hot that we began to complain and could only bear the fire when we wanted it. The mosquitoes began to sting and the snakes to crawl forth, but since then it has been showery and cold, and this morning when I awoke and looked out of the shanty window it was snowing fast. Here [it is] 16th May, but now Mrs. Elliott says we may expect warm weather after this.

We, i.e., the boys and I, are quite busy at our gardening. We have cleared quite a bit of ground and planted quite a few seeds and plants, so if we have not much else we expect to have a quantity of vegetables. The soil is very rich and easily worked. We have got in a nice patch of peas, some onions, cress, radishes, lettuces, beets for pickling, parsnips, carrots, and a great many cabbage plants. [We are] now preparing for potatoes. If we should have more than we want, we can make a good price of them at the mines, also any other farm produce. That is what makes this part so much better than it used to be. The iron mine is very rich. And we have tomatoes, cucumbers, and watermelons to plant yet. I begin to like gardening. It is nice to know the land you cultivate is your own.

David might have sold this place, but people tell him in 4 or 5 years it will be worth a thousand dollars. People are flocking in round the mines fast. I believe in a few years it will be quite a town. The railroad will soon be completed.

The school is opened now where we go to church service $4\frac{1}{2}$ miles away. If we could spare the boys, I should like them to go, as there is a master, but David says they are as good as a man. They are good boys, they work regular hours, so we get on. So we have made the place look different since the snow went away. I can tell you it is very healthy being out in the air all day. The boys, and girls too, grow fast.

They have been making themselves a set of dominoes during the wet weather. They wanted me to make them a game on cards, such as I have told them I used to play at the Rectory with Miss Lillie, but I advised them to ask their Grandma to buy them a game and send it to them if she can and will. However, they did not like to.

David and I went to church service on Sunday and Arthur went with us. Poor Edward is grown out of his boots and we cannot get him any more just yet, as we shall not feel happy till we are out of debt. The children all round go barefoot all the summer, and most of the women too, Mrs. Foster and Mrs. Hewton and all other Canadians.

I don't think Mrs. Elliott does. Her father was a gentleman, an Irish gentleman who married his first wife's maid, Mrs. E's mother, and was old enough to be her grandfather. He is dead and she is married again, a Canadian, a drinking man. Her first family will not have much to say to him, they are all grown up. I know her, she puts me in mind of Miss Gough of years gone by in her talk and manner. David boarded there till I came. Mrs. Pilgrim told me that Mr. Lloyd, her first husband, was a gentleman. There is money which they all come to as they come of age.

I commenced to tell you of our going to service, only this rigmarole came into my head and oozed at the end of my pen. It was a nice day and I enjoyed the walk. The hills were not so bad to climb now that the snow is off them, and the birds singing, the wild flowers peeping, and the cowbells ringing, made it all pleasant. We got there just as they were commencing service.

The usual congregation was there, not forgetting the babies and dogs, one of which decidedly disapproved of our singing and set up a doleful howl.

The service was nice, the old familiar words in that strange out of the way place seemed like the voice of an old friend speaking. Mr. Schammel is a good extempore preacher. After service there was the usual handshaking. Mr. and Mrs. Payne would like to have had us go home with them, but as we had before promised to their daughter, Mrs. Orr, there we went. They are nice people. Two little children and the old people, Mr. and Mrs. Orr, live with them.

The schoolmaster also lodges there. It is a double shanty, part of it being partitioned off into two little bedrooms and two beds in the living room. Everywhere as neat as wax; the boarded floor, clean and nice, the stove and its accompanying pots sending forth a savoury smell, the walls, as is the custom here, covered with newspapers and little pictures distributed about, a long white table, etc. etc.; i.e., I felt at home. I always feel so wherever I go. I believe people like it.

Mrs. Orr is very nice. The old people are English, at least he is. I am not sure about old Mrs. Orr. I asked him how he liked Canada. He has been here thirty years; said he would like to go over and see the old country, but he would not go back there for all he could see.

The schoolmaster is also an Englishman, by name Emmet, a nice young man. We got into a chat. He likes the country very much, has been out about a year. I asked him how many children he had, how many do you think? – 8. I told him he had easy times. He tried to prove to me he had as much to do as if he had more, but I did not seem to see it.

We had a famous dinner, to which I did ample justice, my walk having made me ravenous. [They served] stewed chicken, mashed potatoes, and custard pie, i.e., custard flavoured with ess[ence] lemon on a short crust, on soup plates, and the whites beaten up and put on the top. You had better try it, it was very good.

I looked at Mrs. Orr's bookshelf, and she lent me a book and showed me an album of impromptu verses, wishes, etc., written by her numerous friends. She wants me to write one. So I must, I suppose. I had a laugh over some of them and Arthur and I remembered two to tell you. One was:

To Kitty
"Remember me when far away,
If only half awake.
Remember me on your wedding day,
And send me a piece of cake."

The other was:

"The deer loves the valley,
The fox loves the hill.
The boys love the girls,
And I guess they always will."

Arthur stayed to Sunday School and took his first library book, "The Mysterious Island" by Jules Verne. David and I came on home as we wanted to see Florence. She was well and blooming as a rose. Gertie is staying this week at Mrs. Hewton's.

Edward and Kate, Lily, and Johnny, we left home ... they were all right when we returned. My girls all promise to be very pretty, there is not two alike. Johnnie is a great, fat, blue-eyed boy, in trousers and a waistcoat. He was grown out of his frocks and I thought it not worth while to make any more.

Father would miss his dumplings here. I don't believe people about here make them. I have made them a few times when I have something with them. By the by, I heard a comical story the other day about dumplings. I won't vouch for the truth of it though, so I won't ask you to believe it unless you like.

Some one called in a house where the mistress was making dumplings for dinner. "What are they?" said one to the other. They could not tell. When they were cooked, the good lady took them up and in so doing, let one drop on the floor, which was speedily snapped up by a dog lying near. Finding the dumpling hotter than he liked and sticking to his teeth, he brushed his scalded jaws with his fore paws. "Tell you what," says one man to another. "They're dog's jew's harps."

So the next time Mary makes any, she can call them dog's jew's harps, and with that I'll get into bed, for I'm writing this in my nightdress. Good-night.

Saturday. This has been a nice day. I have been high busy all day cleaning my shanty, baking a nice batch of bread; my bread is as good as the best baker's bread, and the yeast is home made. I shall be happy to send the recipe for making it to anyone who cannot get good brewer's yeast. Heavy bread is unknown.

David is come home for his Sunday, which we count on all the week. He is pleased with what we have done in the gardening line. I forgot to say that I have made a nice Strawberry bed. I had over 100 plants given me. I don't suppose they will bear this year, but there are acres of raspberry canes all round, and scores of gooseberry bushes.

David says they are going to open, as a trial, a mine quite close to us. If it proves a good one and is likely to be worked, it will be a good thing for us.

Give my love to Rosa and Gertie, and Father and Mary, also all inquiring friends. Remember me kindly to Mr. R. Wright. I very much regret that the pictures he so kindly intended to send us were too large. They would have nicely ornamented our shanty walls.

We see a newspaper every week and any news from England of importance is always in, so we knew of the death of Prince Leopold, and also of the earthquake; still any papers are acceptable. I don't know what I should do without the reading you send.

Cousin Bessie has been kind enough to send some lately. I wish you would send them this letter with our kind love and thanks for the "chatterbox." The boys and their Mother too would like to hear more about Pat and Paddy. Now I must say Goodnight and goodbye. I am afraid this will be overweight, but this is the thinnest paper I can get. Love from all to all. Goodbye. God bless you. Write soon.

Sunday. Sweet day; so cool, so calm, so bright. Imagine, if you can, the blue expanse of sky, the bright sun overhead; the woods all round budding for summer, the cowbells in the woods sounding like bells ringing for church. I often think with pleasure that the same sun warms you and the same moon lights you at night; and, best of all, the Same Kind Heavenly Father takes care of us all.

P.S. When Arthur came back from Sunday School, he brought dear Fanny's nice long letter, also the papers and seeds. David thanks William for the seeds very much and will be glad to hear from him when he can write. I will write soon to Fanny. Love to them all.

Many thanks for the British Workwoman and newspapers.

I should think you were pleased indeed to see Fanny. I envy her sometimes. Love to her.

[no signature]

Anna grew deeply concerned about her mother's health, even though she knew there was nothing that could be done about it. To give her mother something else to think about, Anna tried to write interesting letters home describing in detail her neighbours – eccentric, amusing, kindly, helpful – just as she found them. Although shanty life was often hard and the family was forced to live most frugally, Anna was careful not to complain in her letters home, giving more emphasis to the lighter side of their lives.

Every penny had to be considered carefully before it was spent. They soon bought a young pig to raise during the summer for the next winter's meat. They looked ahead, too, towards the time when they could have a cow. Instead of doing everything by hand, they might one day have a team of oxen for the heavy work. These animals also would provide a means of getting to town for supplies, without being dependent on helpful neighbours.

Because Coe Hill was their marketing centre, they became closely acquainted with several families there who admired the honest effort that the Leveridge family maintained in face of hardships, and tried to help them along. David began to board with a family named Blackburn, who lived from the village that grew up around the mines. This was much better than the boarding-house, for the Blackburns also were industrious farmers, anxious to get along.

The store and post office in the village was operated by a kindly couple with no children of their own. Mr. and Mrs. Tivy had moved in from Millbridge with the first settlers. David and Anna had not met them before coming to Coe Hill, but soon grew to value their friendship. As the years passed, seeds were planted that grew into family ties when the Tivys, Leveridges, and Blackburns became closely related through marriage.

Only a part of another letter that Anna wrote home at this time remains.

... same time, but hovers behind you with the teapot and the sugar basin, and heaping this and that on your plate, so you are bound not to starve. She is a very handy old lady and wears but scant clothing in the winter, goes in the snow bare-footed all about down to the barn, she says that she does not feel the cold. In the summer she wears next door to nothing, and may be seen at the wash tub or mopping up the floor, as it was expressed to me, in her shift tails, i.e., in her chemise and barelegged. If any one of the male gender is in sight, she will pop on her husband's coat, or anything else she can find.

Her daughter, a great girl of 15, looks 2 or 3 and twenty, told me she was at a friend's house one day and knew her mother was washing in her shift tails. So she and another girl agreed to dress up and scare the old lady. So her friend put on a pair of pants and a coat and a false moustache. When they walked quietly in, her mother ran up the stairs with a shriek, but finding the girls out, she came down and gave them a good rating.

Thursday Evening. This has been such a lovely day, if it were not for the deep snow and keen, frosty air, one might have fancied it a May day, such a lovely blue sky and bright sun; I have been out all day. I have been to see Florence and Gertie. Harriet Lloyd (Mrs. Elliott's sister, a girl of 17 who puts me much in mind of Rachel Leveridge, as tall and stout, and who is staying till the spring with her sister) went with me.

We went to see Mrs. Hewton first and stayed there to dinner. Gertie is looking well and seems very comfortable. She had no wish to come home, and Mrs. Hewton would have been loth to part with her. They are going to buy her some new boots when they go to the store.

After dinner we went to Mrs. Foster's where Florence is. I had never seen her, but I liked her very much. She is a young woman of 21 or 22. She seems to treat Florence as a young sister, and Florence looked well and well cared for. Mrs. Foster has been educated well. I fancy she was going to be a schoolmistress, but she worked so hard in her young time at outdoor work on the farm that her health was not good enough, to her great disappointment, as she is fond of teaching.

57

She hears Florence read, and corrects her and teaches her, at which I am glad. Florence did not wish to come away and seemed very happy, so I feel more comfortable about her, as they were strangers to me. He seems a very nice man, but the baby is the tiniest I ever saw at 4 months old, mine have all been bigger born. They dress babies so differently here, long sleeves, as in winter they would freeze and in the summer scorch up.

We had a pleasant walk through the woods. The snow is packed hard with the frost that you don't sink in much, and a sleigh and oxen has been backwards and forwards several times. Coming home at sunset it was lovely. As we came on to the clearance out of the woods, the sky was such lovely and delicate colours, pink and purple ... [end of letter].

12

The next letter appears to have been written two years after the family moved to Coe Hill. During that time, they greatly improved their garden plot and enlarged the clearing, judging by the crops produced.

After tending the plants carefully through the growing season, all the family worked at gathering in the harvest. In cutting the wheat and barley, it was impossible to gather every stalk of grain into the sheaves which they tied by hand, folding some of the straw to make a kind of string. The cutting was done by using a cradle; the cradle was like a scythe with long fingers attached to catch the stalks when cut and drop them in a neat pile at the edge of the swath.

It was the task of the younger ones to search carefully over the harvested fields to pick up the heads of grain that broke off or were left behind. Nothing must be wasted, so the fields were gleaned as in the days of Ruth, so picturesquely described in the Bible that Anna sometimes read aloud during family worship in the mornings.

Smaller buildings were soon put up around the shanty area to house animals and fowls. David and the boys working together could make such small log structures themselves. When possible, they were given a southerly exposure, with the doorway on that side. A loft was usually built above to be filled with marsh hay or some of the straw from threshing. The hay or straw insulated the animal quarters below from the cold, as well as providing fodder for use in the later part of the winter when the outdoor hay or straw stacks were used up.

The building of a log barn was anticipated, planned, and prepared for during several seasons. Anna and David also looked ahead to the time when they would be able to build a larger house for their family; but the need for a barn was greater and it would have to come first.

The forming of an Agricultural Society in the district and the holding of a Fall Fair were of definite significance. To David, these events indicated that the farmers around Coe Hill believed in the area's future, took pride in their products, and wanted to learn from each other in the competition the Fair provided. The beginning was small, but the Fair would grow. It indicated, too, that the settlers were intent on making the land produce their living for them. Working in the mines was thought of as a temporary necessity, not a means of making a permanent livelihood.

The building of a school was another mark of progress. The schoolroom served not only for learning but as a community centre: it was a place to gather for worship on Sunday, and for social enjoyment at other times. Located within comfortable walking or driving distance, small country schools or churches were the gathering centres for the residents of each area.

Many of Anna's letters were not dated, which makes arranging them into proper sequence difficult. There appear also to have been several during this interval that have been lost from the collection.

Coe Hill Mines/Wollaston/Hastings Co./Ont., Canada/
Friday, August 28th

My dearest Mother and Father and all,

I think it is about time for another of my rambling kind of epistles, don't you – it is some little time since I heard from you last, our letters generally cross. I had a letter from dear Fanny to-day. Mrs. Elliott was up and brought it. We have three mails a week now instead of one.

Poor Fanny has had something to go through with. I am so thankful dear William is better. I wish he could get something they would like better. How they must miss Ilsing, such a nice garden and everything as they had. I should not like where they are now. How David and I would like to have them here. I wish they had come and taken that place of Mr. Elliott's, but it is no use regretting. No doubt it's all for the best.

We were sorry to hear of poor Sophia's sudden death, it was sudden to us, as we had only just heard she was ill. Thank God we are all well, and going on as usual, and hope that you are the same.

We have had a lovely summer, it is not so hot now, pleasant and sunny most days. Sunday is service Sunday. I think of going, if fine. They have only just commenced again. It is too far in the hottest as well as the coldest of the weather.

We went last Sunday to see Mrs. Foster, our neighbour. After dinner, Mrs. Foster and I went to see her neighbour, Mrs. Mayo. We were the representatives of different nations, Mrs. Foster being Irish, Mrs. Mayo, Scotch, Mr. Mayo, French, and I English, and a young woman there Canadian. It is nice to have nice neigh-bours, though they are so far away.

Monday evening. I started for church yesterday and had only just got into the woods when it began to rain so I turned back, as when it rains here it generally rains in earnest and $4\frac{1}{2}$ miles is too far to go in the rain. I wished afterwards I had gone on as the rain was not much.

To-day has been our harvest day, as Mr. Foster came and cut our wheat. Edward is gone back with him to harvest his oats in return, that is how we do about here.

David is at home now with a hurt leg. A large piece of iron ore fell on it and cut it. It is such heavy stuff that a small piece is enough sometimes to break a man's leg, it is dangerous work. How glad I shall be when he can be at home, but every year brings us nearer to that time. I was told the other day that if every one who came into the country had got on as well as we have, no one need be afraid to come into the backwoods. The Faraday Postmaster was looking round our place yesterday. He said that in a few years' time we might hope, if we had our health and strength, to be very comfortably off.

The boys are getting quite good shots; on Saturday they went to the next farm, Mrs. Peacock's, for butter and brought home 4 partridges, which made us quite a nice dinner, and David brought in several pounds of nice bacon which Mr. Tivy at the store gave him. They are very kind to us. The boys always get quite a good dinner every time they go, and when I go I am al-ways asked upstairs and treated like a visitor.

The boys are going to the store so I must finish this off now, hoping you are all well, and with love to dear Father and you all.

I remain
Yr loving Anna

Coe Hill Mines/Wollaston/Hastings Co./Oct. 4th 1885

My dearest Mother and all

I think it is about time I should write to you again, or you will be wondering what is the reason. I hope you are all well, as we are, thank God. David has had a bad leg, but it is nearly well now. He has been at home these five weeks. A large piece of iron ore fell against it and cut a piece out down to the bone; it was an obstinate place to heal.

He has been busy at home, getting in and threshing the wheat, and the boys and he have built a shed to keep some calves in, etc., etc. He talks of going back to the mines this week. Work, we hear, is plentiful. I wish we could do without, but we cannot just yet, though our prospects improve, thank God.

We have several bushels of wheat, which will be quite a help this winter; and are now harvesting our potatoes of which we have a large crop of fine ones, a great many more than we shall want for ourselves, besides a quantity of fine turnips and other vegetables. We are going to have a pig to raise our own pork.

Our Agricultural Fair is on the 15th of this month. I hope it will be fine. We have several things to exhibit. We are thinking of sending wheat, barley, turnips, parsnips, carrots, potatoes and pumpkins. I should like you to see our pumpkins, we had close to 40, some immense ones that I could scarcely lift from the ground. I shall have to give you a full account of the show. Among the Ladies' Work I shall send a crocheted petticoat which I have made for myself, blue and grey, it is a very nice one.

We have been having splendid summer weather till to-day which is colder. The woods have had on their gorgeous Fall dress of orange and crimson and yellow. Now the leaves are falling and it will soon be time to look forward to our long, cold winter. Thank God, each winter finds us better able to meet it. We do not dread it so much when we are supplied with necessities.

The boys and girls are growing all out of knowledge. Edward will soon be 14 and Arthur 13. They are stronger than I am. Florence is a fine girl. She looks older than she is, and is tall and stout. Her hair is still fair and is getting long and thick. She is reckoned very pretty and takes everyone's fancy. She went to the store the other day and I went the week after. They seemed to think a deal of her. She was weighed there and weighs 80 lbs.

Edward weighs only 68 and Arthur 69 lbs. Edward is not nearly so thin as he used to be. I think the life they lead suits the boys, they say they would not like to be in England again. They are quite good sportsmen; they have shot a good many partridges this season. Sometimes they get three and 4 at a time and they often make us a good dinner. We had to-day a rabbit and a partridge stewed with sage and onions, and a pumpkin custard.

My hens lay well; we have plenty of eggs to use and some to sell. We can only get a cent each, though. I often wish dear Fanny and William had come out where they could have been near us. It would have been so nice to be so near each other and every year you seem to be getting on. We are getting quite a nice clearing now and please God, next year shall have a much larger crop.

It is settled now that we are to have a school built next summer about a mile and qr from us, which is not reckoned far in the backwoods. I don't think the boys will go any more as they are so useful at home. Katie and Lily begin to read nicely for their ages, but it is impossible to have regular lessons at home except in the winter. Now the little ones pick up the potatoes and gather seed and look up eggs, and do a good deal of playing.

Johnnie is getting a jolly boy. He is quick and sharp, and always ready and anxious to help in anything. His Rosie is still in the land of the living, after being drowned and buried alive and hung on a stump and reskinned. Lily's doll's name is Nellie and Katie's Clara. Last Sunday Katie was giving Johnnie a little talking to, and telling him if he were a good boy he would go to heaven. "Do you know what a nice place that is?" said Katie. "You will have everything you want there." "Well," said Johnnie, "I guess I know what I'll want and that is *cheese,* for we haven't had any for a long time." I could not help laughing though I pretended not to hear. Katie grows but Lily is small of her age though she is healthy and strong.

I must finish this off in a hurry as the boys are going to the store. Give my love to Rosa. We got the Crystal Stories on Saturday. Many thanks. Love to Mary and Gertie, Father and yourself. Love to dear Fanny. I will write to her soon. The children all send their love and kisses, in which David wishes to join.

I remain
Yr loving Anna

The railroad north to Coe Hill and beyond was built with three objectives, each of which was achieved for a time. It gave access to the pine forests, provided an outlet for shipments of minerals, and serviced the settled areas. Many years later motor vehicles demanded steady improvement in highways; afterwards the greater flexibility of shipping by heavy trucks, and the use of passenger cars gradually put the railway out of existence.

At first the iron mine at Coe Hill was thought to have great potential. The ore body seemed large and the iron content was good. So the venture started out well and encouraged many settlers to come into the area in hopes of making a good living by working at the mine, or by supplying food for those who did. But the ore proved to be of a more complex nature than the first testing had shown. The quantity of sulphur and other materials present made the smelting more difficult and expensive.

Tremendous quantities of iron ore of greater purity soon were located in the Mesabi Range of northern Minnesota. Being close to Lakes Michigan and Superior, this ore could be transported cheaply by water to the steel mills of the Ohio valley, and the operation at Coe Hill ceased production. Several attempts were made to revive it, but finally it was completely abandoned.

By this time, however, most of the settlers had established themselves firmly in farming and stayed in the district in the hope that they would be able to get reasonable returns from the land. This way of earning their living, supplemented by cutting timber in the winter, was satisfactory for some time. But as the years passed the shallow and stony top soil began to wear out and the crops it produced became poorer and less valuable. A depression in the nineties helped discourage many residents. They abandoned their farms and went to the new lands of the western Canadian plains.

The lumber company that built the railroad into Hastings county brought out vast quantities of beautiful pine logs from the virgin forests. As the stands of trees were cut, the line was advanced farther into the backwoods to reach more of that valuable timber. In counties where rivers were available, pine logs were cut during the winter months and drawn to the banks of a stream to be floated south on the spring flood waters till they reached the lumber mills at the mouths of the rivers.

The Leveridges had settled near the height of land that separated the waters flowing south to Lake Ontario from those that travelled east and north to the Ottawa river. The Ottawa valley became famous through many years for the quality of its pine timber and was the domain of the greatest of the Ontario lumber kings.

The timbering companies secured pine cutting rights on Crown lands from the government. When an area was selected, a group of men with their foreman and cook moved in during the fall. Camps were built to lodge the cutting gang through the winter season. Then, with axes and saws, the slaughter of the great trees began. The mature white pines that had stood for a century or more came crashing down. They were sawn into logs, and then drawn by teams of heavy horses along winter roads cut through the swamps, following streams along the low ground to the railway line. Great pines up to five feet in diameter, standing a hundred feet or more in height, were highly prized because of the wide boards they produced, free from knots. These stands of pine grew in close ranks, free of branches to a great height, where the breezes sighed gently through the spreading boughs. The high hills east of the shanty had been covered with these splendid examples of nature's majesty. It had taken undisturbed centuries to produce such trees: one winter's work by man, and they were gone forever. In their place a tangled mass of waste branches was left to dry through the summer and become a dangerous fire hazard. Great scarred pine stumps still remained for almost another century after the fires were out, providing a mute reminder of the splendour that had been. Gone too, was the thin layer of good soil from the rocky hills – burned away, leaving the crests to be swept bare by winds and rain.

But life goes on. When the fires had passed, a heavy growth of raspberry canes sprang up and flourished for some years until the next phase of growth rotation produced a crop of poplar and white birch trees. The berries were a welcome source of food for the settlers, who enjoyed them as much as did the bears who wandered over the hills.

The railroad continued to serve the settlers for many years after the mines closed and the pine trees were gone. The supplies they needed and the services that it could provide gave it work to do. The winter cutting of hardwood lumber by the settlers had to be moved to markets. Road transportation was slow and uncertain, and the railway was the life-line of the settlers. But at last motor transport left it behind and it became useless in its turn.

A logging camp was established for one winter near David and Anna's home. It was a busy place that season, but was abandoned after the spring came and the pine had been cut. David paid a small sum for the campsite and the privilege of salvaging anything he could use from what the lumbermen had left behind.

Anna tells us about this in one of her letters, of which again only a portion remains. This camp gave her a chance to apply the Golden Rule, and it brought a return of much good to them all.

[the letter begins] ... sleigh bells jingling as you dash up and down the hills.

We have between forty or fifty men in a shanty about two miles from us. But I may as well tell you all about it. You know the Canadian forests are composed largely of pine trees which grow up to a great height, straight and tall, their dark Green branches stretching up against the sky. They are the most valuable of all the trees and are bought up by companies who send gangs of men to cut them down and saw them into logs.

They come into the heart of the woods and build a large shanty and stables and other places. There they live till they have cut all the pine around. They have a boss and clerks and a man cook, they live well. When they first came in they lived in tents for a week or two till the shanty was built. They were not far from us and we often saw them about. Now there is a team go[ing] back and forwards every day, besides people going in and out. So it, comparatively speaking, [is] quite lively.

When they first came in, the cook came to me almost in despair. It was so cold in the tents he could not get his bread to rise. They had big fires and stoves, of course. So he asked me to help him. I told him I would do the best I could for him. He said, if you will, I will do the best I can for you. So I baked every day for him till he got himself round. I baked close to 200 lbs. of flour. The men told me they liked my bread.

The cook was so grateful he brought me about 40 lbs. of dripping, enough to last me a long time. He told me to send the boys in sometimes and he would save me some more. There was 12 barrels of pork and 12 cwt. of beef went in last week, so they have plenty of meat.

It is a good thing for us, their coming in here, as they have bought all the potatoes we can spare – about 100 bushels at 35 cents a bushel, that is $1.5\frac{1}{2}$ a bushel, and they come and fetch them out. We had over a hundred cabbages trenched, and they took all them. I don't know what we shall get for them. I asked 4 cents each. I expect they will take our carrots and parsnips. We have several bushels, besides beets. It happened very fortunate for us, as it would have cost us a good bit to get them out to market. They sent word that they were very pleased with the potatoes. I am also all my spare time knitting socks and mittens for them. They will be in here till the spring.

You mentioned about apples. We get them sometimes. David brought some in on Saturday night. There were 22 large ones ... [end of letter].

Coe Hill Mines/Wollaston/April 23rd

My dearest Mother and all

I have not heard from you for such a long time that I think a letter must have been lost again. I wrote about the middle of February to be in time for your birthday, and Florence sent you some of her crocheting, but we have not heard if you have got it or no. I hope you are all well, thank God we are the same, and very busy. Spring has come upon us all at once and we are all hard at work putting in the crops. I have put in 15 long rows of broad beans to-day, so you must excuse my writing if it is rather shaky.

The mines are closed now, so David is [staying] at home now for a time. We were able, thank God, by the sale of the potatoes and other things which we grew last year to lay in a stock of flour so that we might be able to get a much larger crop of all things this year by David staying at home to help.

He and the boys are improving the place very much, making quite a nice garden. He is very much pleased with his land. Everyone thinks it will be a nice place by and bye. We have got 500 lbs. of flour in hand and paid for. A great many of the miners who have had to go quite a distance to seek work would have been glad to be in our place.

Our little heifer and steer (or the boys' rather) have gone through the winter nicely and are growing fast. People say [she] will be a cow next year, and it will be nice to have a cow again. She is a tame, gentle creature and will come and take a piece of bread out of your hand if you call her. Our hens lay well now, we have eggs for dinner almost every day.

This has not been a good sugar year, the snow went away too quickly. I only made a small cake of sugar, but I made a nice quantity of syrup for our oatmeal porridge. But they say when there is not much sugar there will be good crops.

The change is very sudden here from winter to summer. A few days ago we could go nowhere out of the beaten track unless you went knee deep in snow. Now the snow is gone and flowers coming in the woods and so hot in the day that we let our fire out, and sit with all the doors (we have only one) and windows open. We have [had] a new south window put in. It makes the place much more light and pleasant. The boys are getting very useful to their Father, they are strong and helpful.

Florence is at home now, she is as tall as Arthur and much stouter. Gertie is still away. She is coming home tomorrow for a little time. Katie is gone to stay at Mrs. Foster's. They are the nicest people we have round here. He is doing the carpentering work of Mrs. Elliott's new house. It is going to be a very nice one.

I suppose we shall put up a barn in the fall. We bought a quantity of lumber when the people at the shanty in the woods broke up their establishment, enough to floor a barn and shanty too, for what money it cost to fetch it in from Trenton. [So we] were fortunate in that.

You ask if I am any stouter or as stout as I used to be. I don't think there is much difference, as the same dress is my best dress that it used to be; that grey alpacca, and a splendid wearing one it is, still looks nice and smart. Mrs. Pilgrim wrote me a nice letter at Christmas in return for one I wrote her, she was pretty well.

Dr Rosa, I will take this opportunity of answering your kind letter, as I know [that you] always see Mother's letters. I was glad you were well. I suppose next week is your holiday. If you go and see Fanny, I hope you will tell me all about her and all the news. It must be nice to live under such nice people as Mr. and Mrs. Tuson seem to be. How fortunate you were to get into such a nice place.

I suppose we shall soon have a school here. Its site is chosen and they often have meetings about it. When there is one I shall be able to tell you more about how they are worked. Haven't you got any more Crystal Stories yet? I had another year of Family Friends, please thank the kind sender with my kind love, they came as a pleasant surprise. Now I must say Goodbye dear Rosa, with love from all.

Dr Mary, many thanks for your welcome letter. I was very pleased to get it and find you still going on all right. Yours must be a pretty busy life. I would enjoy the music and the practices. My occupations lie quite in a different line now.

70

We are going to have quite a large garden this year. We have planted ½ lb. of onion seed, half of it belongs to the boys, and we have barley and wheat, oats, and heaps of other things to put in. I have got some cabbages and cauliflowers, and brussels sprouts, tomatoes in boxes. They will be nice plants by the time it is fit to set them out. I have also got ... [end of letter].

14

As the years passed, life moved along more easily for the Leveridge family in their shanty home. The clearings grew until they provided much of their living. The work in the mine had provided a start and carried them through until the farm began to return an income. Their dreams for the future had always included the hope that the mine would produce well, that a smelter might be built, that an extension farther north of the railway would bring it past David's door, and that additional mineral wealth would be uncovered. But things didn't happen that way. A good, plain living they had, but the luxuries did not come. Their pleasures had to be from simple things.

Within a mile or more of the farm, a chain of small lakes nestled in the woods and was drained by a creek that flowed south to become the Deer river, emptying into a lovely larger lake just to the south of Coe Hill. These waters were sparkling clear and from them several varieties of fish could be taken. While not often could a rest be spared from the ever-present work of the farm, David knew that a holiday was never wasted, and organized an occasional fishing trip for the young people.

Anna's letters continue to picture life in the Canadian home.

My dearest Mother and all:

How glad I was to get a letter from you at last. I thought you never were going to write again. I seemed quite disheartened as week after week passed and no letter came.

We got the Family Friends all right, and Rosa's and Mary's letters, as I dare say you have had one I wrote a little time back. I wonder what became of the letters as one if not more must have been lost. I was glad to hear you as usual. We are the same, thank God, and all at home and all busy most of the time.

David is still at work at home. We have got quite a nice garden this year, and if the crops do well, shall have quite a harvest. The high hill in front is coming green with wheat, and in the valley below barley is flourishing, while both hill and valley is laid down in seeds for a pasture for another year.

Then comes a broad strip of peas for the pig, then a large sowing of garden peas for ourselves. If we cannot sell them green, they will make splendid pea soup in the winter. Then I have a large piece of beans for use both green and dried, as well as several long rows of broad beans. Then comes a large bed of onions, half belongs to the boys. We can make 4 shillings or a dollar a bushel of them. Then I have beds of parsnips, carrots, radishes, and lettuces, and my strawberries are in blossom. Behind the shanty is a little piece of clover sown last year which keeps our pig. It is getting quite a big sow, and I hope will have some young ones this year. Then we can rear some up to kill. We shall have plenty of garden stuff to keep them.

I have some flower seeds coming up in front and am going to plant out this week a large bed of tomato plants, and cabbages, etc. Florence and I put a good many of the things in, so you see we are not idle.

I am doing my neighbour's washing now, as she is not very strong and her sister is married. She finds me in milk and butter.

They keep three cows. I find I am able to do a great deal more than I used to do. I enjoy good health, thank God.

I have no fear, please God, but that we shall get on. David and the boys work well together, he is very pleased with them. Edward is much the strongest. Arthur is not quite as tall, but they are both good boys. Arthur made me a good cupboard in his spare time. Of course it is rough, but I find it very convenient. It stands on the floor and reaches to the top of the shanty, open shelves at the top for dishes, and the bottom closes up and will hold all my bread, butter, etc. away from the flies and dust. The boys are both very handy in that way.

I was surprised to hear Gertie was out again. I think she had a good situation as "Mother's help" at home, and I cannot think how she could go and leave you as helpless as you must be. I am glad that she did not come to Canada if she is so restless, she never would have been contented here. If you have not the spring of contentment within, nothing can satisfy for long in this world. I wish, though, that she had not written anything about it, as I wrote to a lady in Belleville who wrote to me the other day to ask about her. I believe if she had come, she would have helped her. She also wrote to say she heard the mine was stopped and wanted to send me a package. She did not say of what. I shall see when I get it. You see I have friends here.

We were very much disappointed because Mrs. Smith is not coming out. We counted on her coming back. I shall be glad of the Leisure Hours indeed, as we have no reading now. Mrs. Smith is most kind. Give my love to her and thank her. I remember when she lived near us and Ellen Bray and I were girls together, eating her lumps of sugar down in her kitchen; she used to give us some. What changes have come since then!

Give my love to dear Father. I was glad to see his handwriting again, even if it was only the address on the envelope. We are having hot weather now. People are prophesying a hot summer; it seems like it. Everything is fresh and green in the woods. I wish you could see it all.

I am glad Fanny seems to like Norwich. I should like it for a good many things, but should not like to change now. We enjoy a great many comforts we could never have had.

We are troubled with the mosquitoes terribly this spring. They swell and turn red on me till I am all over lumps. They are horrid things. We often have to make a big smoke to drive them away for a time. This is the worst time of the year.

Monday, May 24th. I must try and finish this to-night as I may get a chance to post it tomorrow, but I am rather tired as I have been busy washing all day. We have had a big burning going on to-day, clearing another large piece of ground. It seems a pity to burn up what in England would be valuable timber, but the ashes do a great deal of good to the land. We shall soon be busy planting potatoes.

Give my love to dear Rosa and Mary and Gertie when you write, also dear Fanny. I am counting of hearing how they get on. Has William found anything else to do yet? besides the post office. We had a nice letter from Hannah on Saturday, and one from Mrs. Milk the week before, containing some of Georgiana's wedding cake.

Now I must bid you Goodnight, dear Father and Mother, hoping to hear again soon, and that the course of our letter writing may run smoothly after this. David and the children join me in wishing you love and kisses.

Yr loving Anna
God bless you all

Coe Hill Mines/Wollaston/Hastings Co./Canada/July 18th

My dearest Mother and all,

I must take the opportunity of commencing an answer to your last which I received a little while ago, though I do not know when it will be posted for this is such a busy time and the boys do not go out to Coe Hill unless they are forced. I was glad to get your letter and find you are all as usual, as, thank God, we are.

Also, many thanks for the Leisure Hours, which we were glad to get. Please give my love to Mrs. Smith, and thank her for sending them to us. Our neighbours are glad to borrow them. All papers that we have go the round. When will we get the rest of the "Sundays at Home"?

I was surprised at receiving a letter last week On Her Majesty's Service. What do you think it was? You remember that last letter of yours, which you wrote soon after your birthday and I did not get? It came in the "Oregon," that you remember was wrecked in the spring. "It had 598 mail bags in it, and was wrecked off Fire Island, U.S., on the 14th March, and this letter was found in a mail bag deeply embedded in the sands on the beach near Cape Hatteras, North Carolina, the bag having drifted upwards of 400 miles from the scene of the wreck. 280 out of the 598 mail bags have been recovered."

This word was sent me in a letter from the Post Office Inspector, Kingston, and he forwarded me the lost letter at the same time, all stained and washed by the waves, but still quite readable. Gertie's letter was there too. I shall keep them as a curiosity. I was quite interested to read it after so long a time.

I had a nice long letter too from dear Fanny, which I was so pleased to get, and am glad to find they are doing as well as they are. I will write to her soon. We are still going on all right. David is at home. He and the boys are earning 12 dollars at cutting out a new road in the forest, which will help us to some more flour so that we can jog along a little longer. Our crops are looking very promising, thank God. We are commencing to have a plentiful variety of vegetables and bushels of raspberries are ripening all around. We can have them now at all meals for the trouble of picking. I shall not be able to make the preserve I did last year for the want of the sugar (we have had to do without all except necessaries, to keep out of debt now David is working at home), but I shall dry as many as I can.

We have had some nice strawberries in our garden and shall have quite a quantity of currant bushes after a while. All small fruit does well, it seems natural to the country.

I wish you could look round to see the wheat on the hill and the barley in the valley, and the peas loaded with pods and blossoms. We have a flourishing plantation of cabbages, etc. I have some splendid tomatoes now in flower. How did you make your tomato ketchup that I remember eating in Harleston? ... [end of letter].

[letter begins] ... please send me word next time.

Our sow, we expect to have some pigs in about six weeks. We shall raise most of them if she does well so we can have our own pork. She has not cost us a penny to keep yet. Our young heifer we hope will have a calf in the spring. We have got quite an addition to our clearance since David has been at home, and have a good acre in potatoes, which are looking well. The girls and I put them all in mostly. Florence is staying at Mrs. Foster's for a little time.

The boys are well and busy most of the time. Their Father lets them have a half day sometimes, and they all go to the lakes and fish. There are some lovely lakes in the woods. When the shanty men were cutting wood here, they cut roads to the lakes so that we can go and see them. I have been to two. One is Otter Lake, about a mile off; a large piece of water with trees growing quite down to the water's edge, clear and blue; it is a beautiful place, only so lonely. The boys get lots of small fish, which are nice fried in butter. There is a place, too, about 4 or 5 miles, where they get salmon trout. They are splendid, pink inside. They have been two or three times there, so we have had some fish this spring.

Mr. Elliott gave us half a deer the other day. It lasted us quite a while; I cut off all the meat off the bones in slices, and sprinkle with salt, and put down the cellar, and stew up the bones into broth. Our hens have done well this year and we have over a score nice chickens. We don't keep many as they do so much mischief in the garden till it is fenced in well. I have some nice flowers in front, the air is fragrant with them.

Thursday evening. I must finish my letter or I will not have it ready by the time the boys go out on Saturday. Yesterday we all took a day in the woods to go berrying. We took pails and a loaf of bread for dinner. David and the boys took guns and we had a couple of dogs. We did not go very far from home. It was a splendid patch, as you may know when I tell you we gathered 120 pints, besides what we ate with our bread at dinner. You can imagine how they grow wild in this country. I am drying them on boards on the top of the shanty. I might get $2\frac{1}{2}$ a qt even here for them. We were asked to pick 100 qts at that price to-day, but this is such a busy time. David is cutting some hay, so we cannot spare time; besides, we want them ourselves.

We had the doctor, a visitor to-day. He wanted David to go out in the woods with him, but he [David] wanted to cut some hay. Eddie did not care to go, so Arthur went. They did not see any game, however. Came in and had a cup of tea, etc. at noon and went off again. He is a nice gentleman, though if you met him I dare say you would not take him for one; an old faded woolen shirt and a slouch hat and his pants hitched up with a piece of string. He is an Englishman: people say the son of a lord. I don't know if it is so. He paid me a great compliment when he was attending Mrs. Elliott. He said: "Mrs. Leveridge, you are a credit to our country." I don't know what he meant.

What do you think we had for breakfast this morning? You'll never guess. Don't be frightened – *boiled bear.* How would you like that meat? The doctor picked the bones at dinner. You will say we have strong stomachs, but it tasted like tender boiled pork to me. Mr. Elliott killed two cubs this week and I cooked the legs of one. The rest was given to the dogs, which we regretted when we found it was so nice.

We went to the Sunday School picnic the other day; 25 cents a couple, eat all you like, the proceeds given to the minister. It was held under the trees in the wood. Bread and butter and leg of pork (they called it ham, but I didn't), cakes and tarts, and two seed cakes, and tea, etc. You would have laughed to hear the backwoods speechifying, which was part of the programme, most of the spokesmen unlearned men.

Mr. Payne, a diminutive Englishman, got up on a chair and said, "I's a little man, and I'm going to make a little speech." He brought forward a young man, a new settler who had been appointed superintendent of the Sunday School, and called upon him to speak. All he could say was that he had been made superintendent of the Sunday *Schule* and he wasn't fit for it. I enjoyed the day, however. We called in at Mr. Hewton's and had a nice supper of salmon trout that he had just brought home. Now as it is bed time, I will say goodnight, and bless you all.

I must finish this letter up now. You will wonder why I had not written. Mrs. Elliott is pretty well now, so she does her own washing. One has to be obliging in these backwoods. I have no doubt she would do the same for me, we get along very well together.

I knew that Mr. Breeze, who gave a library to Hochering. He came to tea at the Park.

The children hope there is a parcel post to Canada. It will seem to bring us nearer than ever. Give my kind love to dear Father. I hope he is well. Also to Rosa and Fanny, Mary and Gertie, and with love from all to you all.

I remain
Yr loving Anna

Coe Hill Mines/Wollaston/August 8th

My dearest Fanny

I think it's high time I answered your long letter which I was so pleased to get. I should have written before but I wrote to Mother about a fortnight ago and knew you would see the letter. I was so glad, dear, to find you were going on so well as you are. It is great blessing to have a home and food and clothes from day to day, and I hope that as time goes along it will see you in improving circumstances. You have a great many things to be thankful for, old friends around you, and living so near a church and school, things which we feel the want of very much.

I am glad the dear children are getting used to a city life. Give my love to the darlings and kiss them all for me. I often think about them and look at their pictures. If they are grown as mine are, I should hardly know them now, I dare say. I am glad dear Ernest is such a good boy. Give my special love to him and tell him I am glad that he is keeping the commandments with promise; as he grows older and mixes up with boys and young men of the city he will find much temptation to sin that others in this lonely backwoods life escape. Tell him to be strong and take none but his Captain's Orders and He will see him safely through.

Freddy's nice letter gave his little cousins great pleasure. I think perhaps he would feel somewhat bashful with my big girls. I suppose Mary is still at Harlestone. I often wonder how they get along, I wish I could hear a little oftener. I see by our newspaper there is a parcel post established between England and Canada, which will be a nice thing if they don't make it too expensive.

We are getting on nicely and are all well, thank God. David and the boys have just earned 12 dollars at cutting out some on a new road, which will buy us some flour. We have plenty of vegetables of different kinds. Our crops look wonderfully well,

I am glad to say. We had the minister to see us the other day. He was pleased to see our place looking so well.

We have quite a quantity of dried raspberries, more than a bushel. They will last us all winter, as a few swell out when stewed. We are now drying some rhubarb in the hot sun. It will dry up like sticks and keep so.

We have had a splendid time at raspberries. Besides all we dried, we had them once or twice a day at meals, and the children eating them all the time. They don't seem to hurt them in the least. What would your dear children say to have such feasts? I wish they could share in them.

Now the gooseberries are turning ripe. We got a quantity last year, and away in the woods there are huckleberries and long blackberries, which are both splendid fruits. As Mr. Scammel, the minister, said, this is a country of rude plenty.

We finished to-day ... [end of letter].

Coe Hill Mines / Friday night / Oct. 15th

My dearest Mother and all

I was so pleased to get a letter from you once again, as I had begun to feel quite anxious knowing you were sick. I am so glad your health is better, but grieved that you should suffer so much. It is indeed a rough road that the Master is leading you along, but if His hand is holding you up, you will see His Blessed Face at last, when all pain and suffering will be forgotten in the freshness of eternal youth and strength.

I am so glad that dear Father and all the rest are well. We are all well, thank God. I should have written before, but I thought I would wait till after our Show (which was on Tuesday last) and then I could tell you all about it.

You will be pleased to hear that we got on first rate. We took 18 kinds of vegetables, etc. for exhibition and gained *13* prizes; several first prizes, some second, and some third. I got first prize for my tomatoes, 1st on onions, 1st on carrots, etc., etc. The settlers round were somewhat afraid of us, we had a splendid lot of vegetables. We had a good many people come to look round our garden. They said there was not another like it round the township.

My flowers have been lovely. I had some of the most beautiful Asters I ever saw. When the other flowers went off, I sent bouquets for presents to friends, and they went to cheer the sick, and even were buried with the dead. For Mrs. Foster's little baby died and I sent some flowers to put in its coffin. Poor Mrs. Foster felt the baby's death very much. I went to the funeral. It was buried on their own place in sight of the house. There is a burying ground but people are sometimes buried on their own place.

There was no clergyman. He lives 15 miles away. They wanted me to read the service, but as there were several men present, I said I thought it would be better for one of them to do it. So one of the neighbours read it as well as he could, which was not very well.

Mrs. Elliott has been very ill, but is getting well now. She was sick a good while and then had a miscarriage. There was only I with her besides her husband when it happened, as it was in the night and it came on suddenly. He had to hold the light for me to see to do what was necessary. So, you see I happen with some strange experiences. If anyone had told me I should have to do such a thing, I should have thought it impossible; she was very weak and low afterwards. Her mother came and stayed a fortnight. We thought she would not recover. She looked awfully bad, but she is getting able to get about now, though still weak. I combed her hair for her the other day. She had been too weak to have it done, and it was got in quite a matted state. It took me 4 hours to get it out. If I had not done it, she must have had it all cut off.

My two big girls are away from home now and I suppose will be away all winter. I went to see them last Tuesday, and they are both very comfortable. They are treated as one of the family and have no more to do if so much as they would have to do as if they were at home. Florence is at Mrs. Blackburn's where Gertie was last winter. David is lodging (he is at work at Coe Hill now). I stayed there all night on the Show Day. They are very nice people. Florence has a little bedroom to herself. They have bought her a warm flannel dress for the winter and a pair of boots. Mrs. B. gave me a large roll of butter to take home with me.

Gertie is at the master of the mines, a Mr. Johnson, an Englishman. I went to see her also. I could see at first glance that she would learn nice ways, and Mrs. Johnson seemed to be a nice woman. She is a friend of Mrs. Tivy's. Gertie has not much to do but mind two little children. It makes a difference not having to maintain two such hearty girls, and they get the best of living, plenty of milk.

I had a nice time at the Show Day. David and I were at Mrs. Tivy's to dinner. They are extremely kind to us. David goes to dinner every day there, and Mrs. Tivy gave me a nice piece of material, a kind of cloth which will make Arthur a jacket and Johnnie a whole suit. It was a piece that he had had in his store for a long time.

For the evening, I went to old Mr. and Mrs. Blackburn's, Mr. Blackburn's father and mother. They live a little way off them and are very comfortably off and have a nice home. They have a splendid organ, the best I ever played on here. I wished I lived a little nearer. I might have their daughter for a pupil, and have a good chance of practice myself.

I had my larder replenished tonight, for Mr. Foster walked in a little while ago with a fine qr of venison, as fat as mutton. I wish you could have some. The boys have shot over 70 partridges already, so you see we get a taste of good things.

Sunday Evening. I must finish this letter to-night for David to take to the post in the morning. Now we begin to know people, we have very often Sunday visitors, which I don't much like as it seems to spoil the Sunday. These last three or four Sundays we have had company, either to dinner or tea, and don't get much time for a quiet read.

Last Sunday was so hot we had to sit with open windows and door, and to-day we have had some snow, so changeable is this climate. But we do not experience such severe storms as they do in the States. We have had nothing of the earthquake here. I am getting used to the heat and don't mind it. When it is hot we leave off some of our clothes. I have seen Mrs. Pilgrim with nothing on but a chemise and an old cotton dress on.

We shall soon be looking for our long winter now. The trees are all bare, but we may have some warm weather yet. We have bought another steer this fall, so we are getting some cattle. We shall soon have a yoke of oxen and a cow. At least, the steers belong to the boys, they are grown well this summer. We have a great many very fine onions. We are selling them at a dollar a bushel. We have several bushels, and some very large cabbages.

David is working at the mine now for a while. They are sending out the ore. There is a talk of the mine opening up again.

We had a quantity of tomatoes. I gave away several pecks, and made sweet pickles and ketchup, and the children eat them raw. We did not care about them at first, [but] we all like them now. They are nice sliced up and just sprinkled with sugar. They are reckoned very wholesome things.

I must finish off this letter by crossing to save the postage. I cannot get any foreign paper here. Give my love to dear Gertie, and thank her for her letter. I am glad she is at home again. Also give my love to Rosa. I got her letter on Saturday. She must please take this in answer, I was glad to hear from her. Give my love to Fanny. She does not often write. Also to Mary, I hope she is well.

There was a very nice brass band at the Show, came up by the excursion train. It was quite a treat. What a strange mixture of a life we live here in the backwoods. One day we hear the wolves howl away in the woods, and soon after see an excursion train come in and hear a brass band play.

Thanks for the Sunday at Homes. I have not heard from Greenwich for quite a while.

Now I must conclude with best love to dear Father and you, dearest Mother. I often think of you.

Yr loving Anna

Coe Hill Mines/Wollaston/Hastings Co.

My dear Cousin Bessie:

Many, many thanks for the kind letter which I received from you on New Yrs Day, and also many, many thanks from the children as well as myself for the parcel of books etc., which came at the same time. The children's trust in you remains unshaken; they seem to think a package of books from you as much a part of Christmas as plum pudding and Santa Claus is. It is very kind of you always to think of us away in these lonely backwoods. Reading comes so very acceptable, especially at this season of the year when we are shut in as it were by the deep snow and can only go here and there in the tracked paths. It does not matter if the papers are old or new, they are new to us; and our neighbours are just as eager for them as we are.

I wish you had told me a little more about the wedding. I will just tell you what I know, then you will know all I don't know. Mother said Cousin William was to be married this Christmas, and perhaps one of the girls, and that is the extent of my knowledge. Who the bride is, and all the rest of it I have to fancy.

We had a happy Christmas, thank God. The girls came home on the Thursday till the next Tuesday. Christmas Day was a pet day, as they say here; clear blue sky, bright sunshine and sparkling snow, cold enough to make a roaring fire in the stove very

84

comfortable. We had a big plum pudding, and a chicken, and pork of our own raising. We had a pk of apples sent to us, and some nuts and candies, and we all put our cents together and made some toffee, which is always our high treat on state occasions. So we did very well. The little ones hung their stockings up and put little presents to each other in, and found some nuts and candies in them in the morning.

Florence and Gertie are living away from home now, as I dare say you know. My young ones are all getting so big that when they are all at home the shanty is not big enough. So we are glad to have them away where we know they are well treated. They do not get any money, but are treated as one of the family, fed well, and have nice bedrooms to themselves, besides having more new clothes bought for them than they could have at home. It is a help to us to have two such hearty girls away, though I had rather have them at home, and when we have cows and more to do, I shall have them at home again. They are very young yet. They go to Sunday School together, which is nice for them.

I don't suppose you would know any of the girls and boys, they are grown so much. Edward is 15 and Arthur 14. They are a great help to their Father. I don't know what we should do without them. They have been trying to break in their little steers, trying to get them used to the yoke, so that they can begin to be useful. I hope my little heifer "Daisy" will give milk in the summer, then I shall have the pleasure of making my own butter.

Katie and Lily are my little maids at home. Katie promises to be a lovely woman. She has large brown eyes, and hair dark auburn. She is a lively girl, full of fun, and very affectionate.

Lily is the youngest girl. She will be eight in April, but does not look more than six, she is so small of her age, but she seems perfectly well and strong. She has dark eyes and hair, not such pretty features as Katie's. She is the least trouble of any child I ever knew, I rarely even scold her. She is fond of reading her little books and hymns. She is so pleased with those leaflets you sent in your letter and is learning them. I think she is one of the dear Saviour's little lambs.

Johnnie is my *youngest*, a merry little rogue, and his Father's pet. He will be six in March. He can tell you all the different trees in the woods better than he can learn the letters in his spelling book, and can chop down a tree with his little axe better than he can make a round O on his slate; but there is plenty of time.

I hope we shall have a school as near as $2\frac{1}{2}$ miles built this year. We are going to have the railway near us. It will run quite close to our lot. They have surveyed it and are now about to commence to make it. The station will be about 2 miles off, so we will not seem so much in the backwoods. Save up your farthings and when I get a house up and a dairy of cows, come and stay a while in these backwoods. There you will see the wild beauties of nature to perfection. Fancy such a scene as we see sometimes now. As the sun rises, all over the fields of pure, sparkling snow, and in the background the firs bending their branches with their burden. The maples, beeches, and other hardwoods are coated with ice ... [end of letter].

Eventually it became clear that the mines at Coe Hill would not reopen nor a smelter be built. The railroad further north, first planned to go along the stream that drained the small lakes adjacent to the Leveridge farm, was built some distance to the east. When the heavy stands of pine were gone from near David's property the company decided to put its line closer to other such timber, and another hope vanished.

The settlers kept on developing the land to supply much of their needs. Eggs and butter were traded at the store for groceries. Hewing railroad ties from cedar or hemlock in the swamps during the winters when farm duties slackened brought in a small amount of money.

If a settler faced a job that required more labour than his own family could provide, the neighbours were invited to help; they all pitched in together and held a "bee." There were bees for barn-raising and house-building, quilting bees, logging bees to clear the fallen timber from a winter's chopping and roll the trunks together for burning. Bees helped a sick neighbour put in or take off a crop or cut his winter's supply of wood. The settlers gathered promptly when the call for assistance came. Their own turn to receive might come at any time.

Bees were jolly occasions, for the men competed good-naturedly with each other in the work to be done. Some women came and helped with the meals, for always the settler provided his best at noon and night to feed the hungry men.

David's family in England had been moderately well-to-do. He had several immediate relatives, most of whom were older than himself. From time to time, as these people passed on, small legacies were forthcoming from their estates. The amounts received were not large, but often the money was sufficient to clear off unavoidable debts, or to provide some comfort sooner than possible otherwise.

In 1887, Queen Victoria reached her fiftieth year on the throne, and all her scattered subjects wanted to celebrate. The English, far and near, marked the event in many different ways. The Leveridge family declared a holiday in the backwoods and went fishing.

One of Anna's long and newsy letters mentions the event.

Coe Hill Mines/Wollaston/June 16th

My dearest Mother and all,

I want to write three letters in one, so this will have to be a long one. Dear Rosa and Mary must please take this as an answer to their kind letters which I was so very glad to receive. It will suit me better than writing three separate ones. First, then, I am glad to hear that you are all as usual, as we are, thank God, and going on still the same as when I last wrote, hard at work. David is still at home, very busy.

We still keep hearing about the coming railway but it has not commenced yet. There was a meeting yesterday but we have not heard the result. We hear it is sure to go, as they have obtained the bonus and grant of land from the government. We also hear there are to be smelting furnaces up at Coe Hill, to melt the iron ore. If so, it will make quite a place and it will be a good thing for the farmers round.

Our land is turning out good. Our crops look very well indeed. We have a nice piece of wheat, and I suppose we have the best piece of hay for miles round. Of course, it is not a very large field, but it looks well.

I am hard at work planting potatoes, have nearly finished. David and the boys got the land cleared and the children and I put them in. It is a long job. I dare say we shall have 12 bushels or more planted. It will be a good thing to have a large crop of potatoes as they are sure to sell well. We are eating old potatoes now and they are just as good as ever. We keep them in pits in the winter.

I have a nice garden. My tomatoes, cucumbers, melons, and citrons are growing well. Our cow has not calved yet. We do not expect her to come in before the first week in August. She will be rather late, but if she does well we shall have milk and butter for the winter. Butter is very cheap – 6¢ a lb., eggs 4½ a doz. Our cattle are looking very well indeed.

We had a logging bee last week to log up the fallow that David chopped in the winter. There were 3 teams of oxen and 13 men besides David and the boys. I had plenty of cooking, about 23 folks to dinner and supper. I had to set one table out of doors. We got on well, had fresh pork fried and mashed potatoes, buns, rice puddings, rhubarb tarts, besides frying 4 doz. eggs.

We got a nice field logged up, between 3 and 4 acres. We want to get it ready for fall wheat. We have been burning the wood this week. It seems a shame to burn up so much good wood, but there is nothing else to do with it. There is another large piece to do. We shall have that done soon, I suppose.

I had a very nice parcel from Mrs. Shearing a week or two ago. It came very acceptable. There was a good useful dark suit which, with a very little alteration, will fit David. The trousers are a little too long. A long, grey jacket, which just fits me, and a dress and jacket of Miss Elliott's (they are cousins of the Shearings) which fitted Florence as if made for her. The dress was black cashmere trimmed with black silk, made nicely, the jacket light brown figured material trimmed with brown velvet; two or three pretty silk scarfs and bows, gloves – a pr fitted Florence and a pr for me; needles, cotton, hairpins, buttons, a little doll ready dressed, and other toys and picture books; some of Mr. J. Shearing's Canadian and English wedding cake, etc., etc. They are very kind indeed.

Mrs. Elliott (my neighbour) says they used to have boxes of clothes from Ireland when she was a child, and neighbours had regularly boxes from England. I don't know how it was managed. I think they have to be examined at the Custom House at Belleville and the duty paid. No doubt it costs quite a bit.

I have heard no more about the ten shillings. I wrote telling them where to send an order to, to the Madoc Post Office. (Mr. Tivy changed the one we had from old Mr. Milk's money. We had no trouble. It came in a registered letter.) But I have not heard since. It would be no harm to write, letting them know, if they had any difficulty in sending it, that you would send it. I don't like to write again myself.

June 17th. I must finish my letter tonight for I may have a chance of sending it to-morrow. We have been hard at work to-day, putting in the last of our potatoes. We have just got them all in. I think there must be nearly 14 bushels planted. If they do well, we shall have some to sell.

I went to Coe Hill the other day, the first time since the winter. Katie went with me. Mrs. Tivy was quite taken with her, said she had lovely eyes. Her brown eyes and red gold hair, and fair skin make her quite uncommon looking. Mrs. Tivy gave her a new straw hat, trimmed with blue ribbon. We stayed to dinner at Mrs. Tivy's and had some music, and then went down to see Florence. She is looking well. Her father saw her last Monday. She is quite a *young woman.* I often wish you could see her; she is a sweet girl, though I say it. She has long fair hair and nice teeth. She gets on nicely at Sunday School. They are going to have a picnic on the 1st July.

You will be having fine times next week. I wish I could be there; there is to be a great deal done in the towns here, but it will not make any difference to us. The boys think about having a holiday and going fishing. If we get a dish of salmon trout it will be something nice. It is difficult to make a feast without the wherewithal.

Arthur was suggesting writing to the Queen and asking for some of her spare Jubilee money. The boys are both well. They are having their nightly game of cricket with our neighbours' boys. They are nice companions for each other.

Gertie is getting a fine, jolly girl. She puts me in mind of what Rosa used to be. She has sent you some pressed leaves and flowers. Lily and Johnny are like twins. They are brown as gypsies, playing in the sun all day. I have no time for lessons now. The school is building, I believe it should be finished by August.

We have had splendid weather ever since the snow went away.

It was quite hot in May and is very warm now. There is nearly always a pleasant breeze. How I often wish you could see the sights around which I see. It must be tedious not to be able to go out. I wonder how I should bear it, mine is such a busy life that I have no time for fretting. I often and often think about you, but somehow you don't seem very far off me. I don't know how it is. I was so glad to get such a long letter from you, I should miss your letters so. I was so very glad too to get such a nice long letter from dear Mary; best love to her with this, also to dear Rosa and Gertie, not forgetting Father. The children say he must be a funny man because I often repeat some of his funny sayings.

There is a great show for wild raspberries. We are counting on our yearly feasts. My strawberries are just coming on. We have been terribly tormented with mosquitoes and black flies this spring. You would have thought the children had the measles, they were so bitten when the blk flies were so bad. They crawl under their long hair and behind their ears. I often had to take Kate and Lily and wash the blood off them. They are not so bad now. The mosquitoes are very tormenting, sometimes they keep us awake at night.

I must leave off this long letter; this nice thin paper was in Mrs. Shearing's parcel. I remember when I was a wee girlie, as they say here, one time I was offended at something and you wanted me to kiss you and make it up, but I would not. And you said I would one day wish I could kiss you and could not. I often think of that now, and how your words came true.

Now I must say Goodnight and go to bed – with love from David and the children to you all, I remain, my dearest Mother

Yr loving Anna

Thanks for your constant prayers. I value them highly. Farewell.
We got the Quivers all right, many thanks for them. We like them so much.

Coe Hill Mines/Wollaston/Dec. 12th/87

My dearest Mother and all

I was glad to get the long looked for letter. It seems a long time from one letter to another, as it does to you I dare say. Many thanks for sending the Post Office Order, which I got all right, and which comes in nicely for Christmas. I haven't sent it to Mr. Tivy's yet, but I have no doubt he will take it of me.

I am sorry your hands keep so bad. This weather must be very trying to you. We are having much such a winter as you are having, plenty of rain and dull damp weather, not much snow on the ground. It was raining and freezing yesterday so everywhere is as slippery as glass.

We are all as usual, thank God, and going on much the same. David is still at home at work. We had a raising bee since I wrote last, to raise a stable. We had six men. It is a nice large stable, would hold 8 cows if we had them, and a large loft at the top to hold hay. It is nearly finished now. The boys did the chief part of it.

I hope we shall in a year or so have a houseraising. We have some logs out, and are going to get some shingles (which are thin boards of pine like slates) for the roof. It will take some time to get all ready for it.

Florence has left Mr. Blackburn's as they set up keeping a boardinghouse and David would not let her stay. She was at home a week, then Mrs. Tivy sent for her to go there; said she could be there for the winter and go to school. They are very kind, are they not; after that, I think she is going to help in the house and store. I am sure she is comfortable as they are always so kind to all young people. It is nice for her to go to school.

Gertie is staying at Mrs. Robert Hewton's for the winter. I suppose the school will open at New Year's, but I don't think that I shall send the little ones during the winter; it is about a mile and a half away. There is going to be a service there on

My dearest Mother & all

I was glad to get the long
looked for letter, it seems a long
time from one letter to another as it
does to you I dare say. Many thanks
for sending the Post Office Order, which
I got all right, and which comes in
nicely for Christmas; I haven't sent it
to Mr Sivey' yet but I have no doubt
he will take it of me; I am sorry
your hands keep so bad, this weather
must be very trying to you, we are
having much such a winter as you
are having, plenty of rain & dull damp
weather, not much snow on the
ground, it was raining & freezing
yesterday so every where is as slippery
as glass. We are all as usual thank
God & going on much the same

I have been and am still
busy quilt making, blankets
are so dear in this country
that we have to make up
quilts to keep us warm, I take
care of all pieces of cloth out
of old clothes & stitch them on
the machine, line them & quilt
them together & they make warm,
heavy bed coverings, some of the
quilts in this country are very
pretty pieces not bigger than your
finger all joined in patterns.
We are eating flour of our own
raising now & like it very much,
I hope we shall raise enough next
year to last us, till the next comes
we shall not stand at much expense
then; we hope to keep sheep soon
as soon as we get good fences up,
sheep are very profitable to keep.
We have two nice pigs, one is mine,
So you see dear Mother though we
have not much money we have
moneys worth & are jogging along

94

Christmas Day. We have a Church of England minister now. He lives some way off and has a long round of preaching, so he will not come very often. He has been to see me once, but I believe I told you this when I wrote last.

We have lots òf deer around us in the woods, but have not been able to get one yet, but hope to do so before long. Give my love to dear Fanny, I hope she is well. I haven't heard from them for months, she might write now and then. I think I will write a long letter to Mrs. Anderson. I doubt if she could have got my first letter that I wrote.

I have been, and am still busy at quilt making. Blankets are so dear in this country that we have to make up quilts to keep warm. I take care of all pieces of cloth out of old clothes and stitch them on the machine, line them, and quilt them together and they make warm, heavy bed covering. Some of the quilts in this country are very pretty, pieces not bigger than your finger all joined in patterns.

We are eating flour of our own raising now and like it very much. I hope we shall raise enough next year to last till the next comes. We shall not stand at much expense then. We hope to keep sheep as soon as we get good fences up. Sheep are very profitable to keep. We have two nice pigs, one is mine. So you see, dear Mother, though we have not much money, we have money's worth, and are jogging along.

I have no news, so will conclude with love to Father and you and all. Wishing you a Happy Christmas and New Year.

From your loving daughter
Anna

In the early 1890s a serious depression set in, but its effects on David and Anna, at their remote backwoods farm, were moderate. They had learned to do without frills so it was no problem to continue in the same pattern a while longer. Much of their food was now of their own growing and the slackening demand for their extra production caused no serious concern.

The Leveridges continued with their plans for building a new house. Each year saw something accomplished. Choice logs were drawn out of the woods and left in the sun on skids to hold them above the ground where they would season well before being cut to exact lengths and hewn to even thickness. The ends would be shaped to fit together into dovetailed corners. Shingles were bought and stored for the roof, and square nails were purchased and saved whenever possible.

The location chosen for the new house was slightly to the west of the shanty. It was near the brow of a hill that dropped away sharply to the eastward, providing a splendid view over a valley and the distant hills that rimmed Otter and Mink lakes. To the north, a small grove of spruce trees had been left to break the winter winds. A lovely wild black cherry tree growing near by flowered in spring and gave fruit in summer.

The site chosen for the new house was part of the garden area, where the soil was deep enough to permit a good cellar to be dug out under the building for winter storage of vegetables, and keeping pans of milk or cream cool during the summer. David and Anna planned in every detail the house which was to replace the tiny, crowded shanty that had been their home for almost ten years.

But the years had brought other changes; the health of Anna's mother steadily grew worse. This worried Anna deeply whenever she had time to think about it. In honour of her mother's birth-day, Anna composed a poem that is included in one of these letters. The original copy is worn and falling apart at the folds, showing that it must have been carried about and often reread for its comforting thoughts and the reassurance of the power of faith that it carried.

Anna's knack for rhyming appeared again in her daughter Lily, who at one time made a name for herself as a minor Canadian poet. Many of Lily's poems were published, some attracting wide circulation.

The letters to England now showed more confidence in the family's ability to make a living from their property. David and Anna could now look out over ever-widening fields of grain or hay, a lovely garden, and the new barn with out-buildings gathered around it.

Coe Hill Mines/Wollaston/Dec. 4th, 1889

My dearest Mother and all,

I dare say by the time you receive this, you will have been looking for a letter from me. I thought I would wait a while as I wrote a long letter to Fanny and I knew you would see it. I do hope you are better by this time, it must be hard for you to bear so much suffering and helplessness. I am glad to say we are all as usual, except colds. We are having very sharp weather just now, and we have quite a depth of snow which fell last week.

I was out staying at Coe Hill last week and Katie with me. We went on the Tuesday and Edward came out for us on Saturday with the oxen, so we had a nice sleigh ride. We had a nice time at Coe Hill, everything is so comfortable there, the rooms warm and nice, and Mrs. Tivy is almost like a sister. I came home loaded as usual. I will tell you what she gave me, though she does not call them gifts as she says I do a deal of work for her.

There was material for two flannel shirts for David and enough of the same material for a warm everyday dress for myself, the stuff for a dress for Gertie, linings, buttons, etc., and some checked muslin to make her some aprons. I was not to let her know, as they are to be a Christmas present. Then I have some white aprons trimmed with embroidery to make for a Christmas present for Florence. Then I have two clear muslin aprons to make, trimmed with beautiful embroidery, one for Mrs. Tivy and one for myself, besides other aprons, two print ones for Katie and Lily. She sent me some navy blue cloth before to make myself a best dress. So she keeps us supplied. Then she sent some cloth to make David a pr of pants. She is a friend indeed, so generous; she always keeps me in needles, pins, and cotton. They think so much of Florence, and she is getting so useful to them.

Gertie is gone to J. Hewton's today, so I suppose she will be away all winter, but she is not far off. I had a letter from Gertie a few days ago, she is quite well and getting on ... [end of letter].

Coe Hill Mines/Wollaston/Feb. 3rd.

My dearest Fanny

I think it is about time I should answer your welcome letter which we received a little time ago. I think David is going to write to William. He was very pleased to get his letter, which was a very interesting one. I am glad to find you are going on as well as you are. It is a great thing to have a home that you can call your own, and to be able to make a living nowadays when there is so much poverty and distress all over.

We are jogging along much the same, have to be very careful and make the best of everything. We have such good friends in Mr. and Mrs. Tivy. They seem always doing something for us. They are so fond of Florence, and she suits them so well that they do a great deal for her sake. On Christmas Day Florence and little Nello came over and got us to get a Christmas Tree, then they trimmed it with things they brought (Edward fetched them with the cattle). There were presents for all. David had a new woolen shirt and socks, and a pr of pants and vest that were Mr. Tivy's. I had a set of glass dishes from Florence, with sugar basin, milk jug, and a nice little white pitcher, a box of writing paper and envelopes. The boys had new mitts, Gertie a new dress, wool hood, and two nice white aprons. Katy a warm scarf, and Lily a wool hood and scarf and a doll for them, and Johnny some little toys besides apples and candies, and Mrs. T. sent sugar for toffee. So we had a nice time. A few days after, Mr. Tivy sent a large piece of pork, nearly a qr of a pig.

I was out to Coe Hill last week from Tuesday to Friday, had a very nice time though not feeling very well, for I have had La Grippe, which is going all over the world. I don't feel right yet, for I have a nasty cough, and I suffer with my head. Mrs. Tivy gave me a pr of warm lined shoes for the house, new, and some flannel for an underskirt, besides enough flannel to make each of the boys a new shirt. She is generosity itself.

So poor Aunt Jane is dead. Well, I don't think I ever saw her more than once, so I cannot pretend to be more sorry than I am. One thing, the money will come very acceptable. It will help pay off what we owe and put our house up, which we think of doing as soon as possible. We have got most of the logs cut and drawn up, and are going to have them hewed.

David thinks he ought to pay Hannah and Rachel that money they lent him. I know he ought, but as they get the same, and there will be more, perhaps they will not mind waiting. I think David is going to write to Hannah. I dare say you will be glad of the money as well as ourselves.

This has been a very strange winter for Canada, we have very little snow on the ground and have not had much sharp weather, now and then a few days. It is bad for the backwoods, for the winter is the time when work in the woods is carried on, as the snow makes good roads, but not much can be done this winter.

Gertie has been bad with the Grip. She was getting well when she wrote last. She sent me a nice long letter from Rosa which was quite a treat. I am sure it cheered poor Gertie up, for she feels very lonely at times, and she knows the people. I also had a very nice long letter from Mary, which I was very glad to receive, and thank her for it. I was very glad to read about her boy. He must be a lovely boy. I count of seeing his photo. I wish I could have our children taken, but we would have to go to Belleville or Madoc, so it is impossible.

Perhaps you will send this letter to dear Mother, and she will let Rosa and Mary see it with my love, and please accept as an answer to their letters. I hope dear Mother's feet are better. It is a long time since I heard from her, I expect she does not feel able to write. I send her much love with this, and will be so glad to hear again how she is.

Your little boy must be a dear little fellow. I hope he will continue to thrive. Ernest is going to be a tall man. I expect my boys will not be so tall. Arthur does not grow very fast; he would like to be tall, but never mind, they are good and useful boys. I don't know what their Father would do without them. I shall be glad when we have a house so we can make them more comfortable. Edward was pleased with his papers, which we found out after a while came from Norwich. He likes anything funny.

How nice it must be to see the shops and other town sights, though I should not care to live in the city; still, I often picture the windows lighted up, and the market place. I dare say you would be tired of nothing but snow and bare trees, which is all we can see. We can see our neighbour's house, which is some consolation. Some people haven't even that. Still, on the whole, I like the woods. It makes a difference to be able to look round and call the trees and fields our own. I suppose we shall get our deed this summer, I expect.

Give my love to all our friends, Fanny and James Milk, and Robert, when you see them. I often think about old times and what many comfortable days I have enjoyed at Elsing. I used to like going there.

Now I must say Goodnight and God Bless you, with love to William and all the dear children, in which mine join.

Yr loving sister
Anna

Coe Hill Mines / Wollaston / Feb. 20th

My dearest Mother,

I must try and write you a few lines to wish you many happy returns of your birthday. Thank God who has spared you to us so long; though your years have been those of suffering, still no doubt there have been a many blessings. I hope the blessings will be multiplied and the sufferings lessened as time goes on. I was sorry to hear of your feet being so bad, I hope as I have heard no more they are better.

I am writing this from Mr. Tivy's at Coe Hill where I have been since Monday. Mrs. Tivy has been sick with an attack of bronchitis and they sent for me on Monday to come and stay with her. I am glad to say she is much better. She is so delicate that she soon takes cold.

I am glad to say we are all as usual. We have most of us had the Grip but are got over it.

We have had a nice winter, rather more rain than usual but it is good sleighing now. We are getting on with the materials for the house. We think of having it raised before the spring work commences; than the spare time during the summer can be spent at it. Mr. Foster has promised to help all he can, and as he is a carpenter he can help quite a bit. That money will come just in time to help us to fit it up. David will soon be 50, the day after your birthday. How time does fly.

We hope things will be a little brighter this year. There is great talk of the mines being opened and the railway built. And I think a cheese factory is going to be built. Mr. Tivy is going to find the money. It will make things better.

I have not heard from Gertie lately. I will write to-day if there is no letter this afternoon.

I hope to write more next time. Excuse more now as I am not at home, though I always feel so much at home here; they treat me as if I was one of the family.

Florence is looking so well and is so comfortable.

Love to Father and all the girls with much love to yourself.

Believe me
Yr loving child
Anna

Coe Hill Mines/Wollaston/March 16th, 1890

My dearest Mother and all,

I thought I would write to you again, as I wrote such a short note last time when I was at Mrs. Tivy's, that I hardly liked to send it. We thought about you on your birthday and wished you many happy returns.

Mrs. Tivy was much better when I left on the Saturday, they had me sent home. Mrs. Tivy made me a nice present of a rocking chair when I left, a very nice one, almost like a swing. The other day they sent us an immense pig's head and 2 or 3 lbs. of sausages, they are always sending something.

Lily has been staying there since Friday week. She is about the size of Nello. Fanny, in her letter to Gertie, wanted to know who Nello was. She is Mrs. Tivy's niece and adopted daughter. Mrs. Tivy and her Mother are twin sisters. They think a great deal of Nello. She is a nice little girl, very fond of Florence, but rather spoilt.

I hope your feet are better now than when you wrote to Gertie. (She sent me your letter. She seems pretty comfortable, says she does just as she likes.) You must suffer a great deal with your feet; it seems hard you cannot get your rest. I am glad Father and the rest are well. I had quite a budget of letters the other day from Gertie: one from Aunt Howarth, and one from Fanny, besides a long one from herself. I see by the papers there is talk of a universal penny postage; it will be nice, we can write oftener.

We have had a very moderate winter and a variable one, one week we would have a downfall of snow, the next mild rain which would take it mostly all away and leave everywhere coated with ice. We have fresh snow now and another cold snap, which I hope will be the last till the spring opens, for I am getting tired of the winter. We shall soon be busy sugar making, I hope this will be a good year.

We have got all the timber drawn now for our house and some of the lumber. I hope next winter, please God, we shall be comfortably settled in, for the shanty is very inconvenient for a family.

Gertie, my Gertie, will soon be home again; she is spending a few weeks with Mrs. Foster, as her husband is away from home. I had a chance of a good situation offered me for her with Mrs. Shearing's sister, and I should have been glad to have sent her if it had not been so far. But I was afraid to send a girl fresh from the backwoods and never been on a train since she left England as far as Toronto alone. It is 150 miles from here. Perhaps something nearer may turn up by and by. She is only 14 and there is plenty of time. I expect she will go to school this summer, as much as she can. We did think of making her a teacher, but the school closes during the winter months, so there would be a good deal of time lost. I don't know how it will be yet.

Florence was well and getting on well. She is getting a splendid cook. I never eat better bread than she makes, and she makes cakes and pies good enough for anybody. She is a fat little chunk, as they say here, fair and blue eyed.

Johnny was nine years old last Friday. He is something like Ernest, I think, only not so dark. He is a jolly little boy, full of fun. I wish I could have the children's photos taken, but there is no one round here to take them.

They are talking of putting a cheese factory up in Coe Hill this spring, and there is a talk of the mines being opened in July. Edison, the great inventor, has a share in them now, so I think perhaps they will open again. We shall not know anything definite about the railroad till parliament closes.

I don't suppose that we shall have much of a garden this year, as we are going to put the house close to the shanty in the garden. So it will not be any use putting anything in till that is raised. We shall have to plant it with some late crop. We have six little pigs about a fortnight old, and we soon expect our cow in. We shall be glad of some milk again.

I was so glad to see your handwriting again, though I don't know how you write with your pen held so, still it is often held so in this country by good writers. I suppose it is use. Now I must say Good-bye and God Bless You. With much love to you and the others.

Yr loving Anna

To My Dear Mother on Her Birthday

1st verse
Dear Mother with delight I hail the happy day
Which gave you birth,
And wish that many happy days in store for thee
May be on earth.

The years roll on with ceaseless course, and ever still
Time's tide does flow;
How many years you may be spared to us,
We cannot know.

Changes will come on earth, nothing remains the same
Under the sky;
The young grow old, old ones are called away,
Yes, all must die.

Yet not for ever will the sad parting be,
When it does come.
Bright angels beckon us, and one by one
We're taken home.

Home to our Father's side, to mansions in the skies,
Sweet, happy place;
Where Jesus is, that's where we shall with joy
Behold his Face.

Dear Mother, if I should at first be called away,
Oh! meet me there.
To save us, Jesus came; was crucified that we,
Heaven's joys might share.

If blessed angels come for you, that you may lie
On Jesus' breast;
Wait then for me, that we in Paradise may be
Together blest.

A.M.G.

At last the new house was built. The ground floor was divided into two rooms of almost equal size: one was the kitchen which needed to be large because so much activity in a farm home is centred there. The other area became a combined dining- and sitting-room. Both rooms were comfortable and serviceable. The floors were of wide maple boards selected to be free of knots and of even grain. When scrubbed they shone with lovely whiteness, and they maintained their silky, smooth surface through several generations of family life.

The upstairs was partitioned into four bedrooms, not large, but roomy enough to be comfortable. Each had a window that faced east or west, fitted with the small panes of glass that were favoured in many English homes. Two of these rooms were warmed in winter by the pipes which carried smoke from the cookstove in the kitchen and the heater in the living room. The whole house was pleasantly warm in the coldest weather and airy and cool through the summer months.

The ceilings downstairs were not closed in, but exposed the hardwood beams, roughly hewn square, showing the axe marks. Occasional puffs of smoke from the stoves rose to make the beams darker and mellower through the passing years. While the ceilings were low, there was enough height for a tall man to move around freely.

From the first, the building had a truly homey quality, a serenity and peace that some houses never acquire. This may have resulted from the love that Anna, David, and their children gave the place, penetrating the very walls. (I felt its peace during the years that I called it home, long after that first family had gone.) It was home to Anna, blessed by her prayers of hope and thankfulness.

Anna's sisters, Mary and Gertie, came to Canada about this time. Mary and her family made a home in Trenton and remained there, but Gertie came to Coe Hill and spent some time with Anna in the new home. Gertie found a husband in Coe Hill, an immigrant from a good family in England. Harry Boothby and Gertie were married before long and lived in the village, where they opened up a small store that did enough business to provide their family with a comfortable living.

The Boothby store included an array of candies that tempted all ages. Many children came to see and to buy, often accompanied by their parents. A cent would purchase several of some varieties, and the choice of how to spend so much money was one of the big decisions of childhood. The store also carried the essential groceries that a housewife might need, and did a steady business, its doorbell tinkling to call someone from the living quarters at the back to serve the customers.

Across the road to the south of the combined home and store of the Boothbys was an open field, and within it the deserted mine buildings and the shafts, several hundred feet deep, where the miners had once worked. The village never quite gave up hope that the mine would open again one day.

David and Anna marked moving into their new home with the birth of another child. Baby Frank soon grew to be the darling of the younger girls about the home, who took almost his entire care from their mother's hands. All were delighted with this expansion of their family.

Edward and Arthur were grown now to be capable young men, dreaming of one day making homes for themselves. They worked out among the neighbours more and more often and earned for themselves the money that helped to satisfy a young man's wants. Anna knew that eventually the time would come when the boys would strike out on their own. She often mentions in her letters how useful the boys are and how much they would be missed. But soon, Canada's western areas began to call them, and they listened. The free, good level land of the west was a big attraction. For several years this desire to travel farther from home was checked by their father's need for them. But the home-making instinct became too strong. And in the later nineties, Edward and Arthur did go to the West, settling near Emo along the Rainy River in Western Ontario. They found the land easier to clear and work than the hilly and stony home farm at Coe Hill. When Frank grew old enough to be helpful at home, Johnnie followed his older brothers and settled not far from them.

As the settlers in the neighbourhood became better established and cattle more numerous, a cheese factory was organized and built. It was located about a mile beyond the Faraday Church where Anna and David had first attended. Several waggon routes fanned out from the factory to collect the milk each morning except Sunday. The waggon racks had special railings built around their edges so the cans of milk could be lashed into place and stay put when the roads went up and down the steep hills of North Refrew county.

Each farmer participating had to have two or more thirty-gallon cans for the milk. One can was collected on the morning round, and the other returned with whey at the same time. A small platform was built beside the road in front of each house at the level of the waggon, probably about four feet from the ground. The farmer would place his milk on the platform at around six in the morning, ready to be swung aboard when the waggon came along. The previous evening's milking was kept cool in a stream during the night and added to the morning's supply in time to be collected.

The farmer's share of the whey from the cheese-making was returned to him to feed his pigs. If he wanted more whey, he could always get it by visiting the factory himself once or twice a week. Such a trip was a delight for small boys, especially if it were timed so that they arrived at the factory when the whey was being squeezed out and the curd set. A handful of freshly cut, rubbery curd to munch on was a delight that lived long in the memory of any youngster.

Pasture land on the farm itself was only sufficient for the cows to graze at night. During the days the cattle were turned out to roam through the woods and over the hills to the east and north. These hills had been burned bare of tree growth in previous summers and were covered with a coarse grass that provided excellent pasture.

Several cows in the herd carried bells on their necks to make finding them in the early evening easier. The cows followed each other in single file and wore deeply marked paths that wound through the bush and over the hills to the good pasture areas. The animals showed their engineering instincts by making trails that mounted the hills by the easiest slopes and forded the streams where the water was shallowest. These cow-paths were so deeply worn by succeeding generations of cattle that it took many years of disuse for the markings to disappear.

Sometimes towards evening the animals would head homewards of their own accord, but usually someone had to go to find them. It was customary to watch during the day to see what hilltop in the distance was the scene of that day's pasturing, for this knowledge made the evening hunt for the cows much easier. A dog was always a big help in the search and in collecting the herd when found. Occasionally a bear was sighted, but it usually stayed in the distance.

There were times when the cows could not easily be found, if they had decided to lie down and the bells didn't ring. This seemed to happen oftenest if the family were particularly busy and it was late in the evening before they could take the time to bring the cows home. David spent at least one night in the woods after a fruitless search for the strayed animals. He often told of climbing up into the branches of a tree for the night after becoming hopelessly lost in the pitch darkness of the forest. When

110

daylight came, he found that he was no more than a few hundred yards from his own clearing.

The Leveridges' neighbours, the Elliott family, began to be quite prosperous, as prosperity was rated then, and bought a good parlour organ. Anna loved to play the organ, a pleasure she had missed badly since coming to Canada. She started giving music lessons to one of the Elliott girls and taught her own daughters, Lily and Katy, at the same time. The return for this in money was very slim and casual, but it was a great satisfaction to her to have an organ available near her home. For her own girls to have music lessons was an added joy, so that the lack of steady payment seemed of small account. And, indeed, as time passed, Anna was at last able to afford an organ of her own.

Each year the Christmas concert in the schoolhouse was an affair to which everyone went. Anna describes such an occasion in one of the letters that follows. It was natural that she should be asked to provide a large part of the programme. This gave her an opportunity to have her pupils perform in public, which they enjoyed as much as their parents were pleased to have the neighbours mark their accomplishments.

[the letter begins] ... to be hearing about it. We shall move in as soon as we can, and finish it when we can. We can partition it off into rooms as we can. We spend a good deal of our time in the house already. It is cool and airy, and the mosquitoes don't bother as much as they do in the shanty.

Gertie and I used to sit and sew and read in there. I enjoyed her visit, as her health was improving all the time. I missed her very much and hope she will come back for a while anyhow. She says she begins to feel this her home, and the children are all so fond of her.

Our crops are looking well this year, thank God. We have prospect of a good crop of hay, which will be a good thing as I expect we shall have two cows next summer, if they do well.

The boys grow, especially Edward. He is taller than his Father, I think. He has been busy with his cattle for some time. Arthur put the roof on the house and the floor in. I don't know what David would do without his boys. Florence is still very comfortable at Mr. Tivy's. Gertie stayed a week with her. My Gertie is at home this summer. She is a very handy girl, can wash and bake as well as I can. If Gertie stays at Belleville, I shall let her go, I think, by and bye. The other two girls and Johnnie go to school pretty regularly. They have a master this year, quite a young man.

I have done a great deal of sewing for Mrs. Tivy lately, as we have not had so much gardening to do. I have made 15 chemises, six trimmed with embroidery and nine with crochet edging, which I crocheted. Then I made 10 white skirts trimmed with embroidery, etc., and five prs of drawers, etc., etc. She does not pay me in money, but sends me things out of the store, both for the children and dresses for myself. I have not bought a dress for myself for two years. It is all a help and I am glad to do what I can.

We were surprised to hear about Fanny, but not much when we read Rosa's letter telling of their going about Norwich and on the switchback railway, which was enough to make anything happen. I am glad she got over it all right, and hope she is strong again by this time, and that William is better. His work must be very trying to him. Love to them and the children, also love to Rosa, and thank her for my share of the long letter which we got about a month after it was written. I don't know where it went to. Love to Mary, glad to see such a nice description of her boy. He must be a beautiful child. We count on seeing his portrait. Also love to Father, hope he is quite well.

Remember me to Mrs. Barnwell. I am glad she is such a kind neighbour to you. Now I think I must conclude, with kindest love to you, dear Mother, from David and the children and myself.

Believe me
Yr ever loving Anna

Love to little Mary

Wollaston / Jan. 20th/91

My dearest Mother and all

I received Rosa's short letter a few days ago and I take the first opportunity of answering it. I hope long before I had it, you had received one from Gertie and Harry, as they told me they had written. I dare say she told you all about the wedding and about their coming to mine on the Sun after, so I will not say very much about that. We had a very pleasant time. Harry is very brotherly, calls me his dear sister. I like him very well indeed, and I think Gertie may be happy if she likes. I have not been to see her yet, for the weather has been too sharp to take the baby out, but David has been in, and Lily has been staying at Mrs. Tivy's and her Aunt's.

Gertie has an easy life of it now. She gets up about 9, and it takes her about 20 minutes to do her little work, then she has the rest of the day to please herself in. She is not more than 8 minutes run from Mrs. Tivy's and goes in and out there as if she was at home. Mrs. Tivy is like a sister to her, and she has the means to do it with.

Katie is going out on Thursday to stay a week or two, so she will go to see her Aunt and Uncle. They like going there, he keeps such nice candies and chocolate creams. When David went last week he saw two nice salmon trout, a whole cheese, etc. Gertie likes good things.

We have had a very nice winter up to the present, some very sharp days and more snow than last winter, but some days have been lovely, bright and sunny if cold. We find our new house very comfortable and warm after the shanty.

Arthur has been working out since some time before Christmas, at a neighbour's about 3 miles off, so he comes home on a Sunday. He is helping him to cut firewood, or cordwood as it is called here, for sale. Arthur gets 10 dollars a month and his board.

Edward is busy with his cattle, cutting and drawing fence rails, for we are going to have a cheese factory in the spring. We have put two cows in, so we must make fields to pasture them for milking. We shall have one cow for our own use, besides the Sunday milk of three. I hope they will do well. People say these factories are good things for the settlers.

The boys are grown very much lately. Edward is one inch and $\frac{3}{4}$ taller than his Father and broad shouldered, and Arthur is coming up to him.

Florence was home for a few days a little while ago; she was well and very comfortable. I heard from my Gertie a week ago; she was well and getting on well but complained of being homesick and lonesome, poor child, I know what that feeling is. I wish she was not so far away, so we could see her a little oftener.

Katie is my little maid at home. She is growing tall and good looking. She is like a little mother to the baby, nothing is ever too much trouble to do for him. Lily will soon commence school again. She is very quick, she passed very highly last time. The teacher said that he did not believe there were two in N. Hastings who did better. They have a new teacher now, a young lady.

Lily and Isabella Elliott, my little music pupils, are getting on so very nicely. Mrs. Elliott has a very nice organ. Lily goes to practice every day and I give them a lesson once a week. I should get 5 dollars a qr for Isabella, but the money does not come in very regularly. Still, I am not so particular, as Lily learns.

I was so very pleased with the music Rosa sent, and thank her very much for them. They will soon be able to learn them. I should like very much to get some of the music advertised on the cover of the song book. Would it be any use sending you Canadian stamps? I suppose not. I should like to get Jousse's Catechism of music, price 6s.

Johnnie is at home this winter. I did not like to send him for fear he should slip and hurt his arm again. It is growing strong now, he can use it quite well. I don't know if it will ever be straight, though still the doctors said it would in time. He is grown very much.

My baby boy will be half a yr on the 29th of this month. He grows very nicely, has had two teeth a long time before he was five months. He is a good boy and his father makes a deal of him. David is well except for a cough and cold which has been going through the house. I am as usual, getting older. I begin to see a grey hair or two, but there's not enough to notice unless you look close.

We had a nice Christmas. We had an entertainment, or a social as they call it, here at our school house on Christmas Eve and it was quite a success. The school was crowded. It was for the children, who went free. All ladies who provided went free also. Outsiders and gentlemen paid 25 cts each, which money went to buy presents for the children. Most of the mothers baked something. I made 30 little rolls of pork, chopped fine and spiced, nice short crust; and 30 good currant buns. Some made one thing and some another; then these things were divided and little paper bags were filled and carried round, and a good cup of tea boiled in a big sap kettle on the stove.

There was a Christmas tree for the children. We got several things off. Florence put on for us each a very pretty china cup and saucer (it is fashionable in Canada to have all cups different).

She also sent me a nice gilt frame looking glass for my bedroom. Katie and Lily had each a nice bible, and Johnny a warm scarf, etc., etc.

Mrs. Neal had her organ there. I played the Overture to the Caliph of Bagdad and sang the song "Who will care for Mother Now?" Lily and Isabella played and sang some Christmas Carols, helped by Katie. They played very nicely. Lily also sang and played "Driven from Home." Mrs. Payne, a neighbour of ours, sang "Dame Durden," which was very nice.

It was a lovely moonlight night. We shut up shop and all went, took the cattle, and had a nice sleigh ride. Baby was very good; there were lots of babies there. Florence and Nello rode from Coe Hill with others.

I was sorry to hear, dear Mother, of your feet being so bad. You must feel this cold weather very much. I hope Father is better. Love to dear Rosa and Mary and Fanny. I hope they are well.

We have had lots of meat this winter, more than we ever had before. Did I tell you about Arthur shooting 4 deer? I think I did. We killed 4 pigs too, [for] the house, 1 large one and 3 smaller ones. I think perhaps I have told you all the farming news though, but I forget from one time to another.

Give my love to dear Cousin Bessie and thank her very much for the books she sent and the lovely cards. The children were very pleased. I will write as soon as I can, but I have not much time to spare. Now I must stop, I suppose, as I have come to the bottom of my sheet. Love to you, dear Mother, and many kisses from

Yr loving Anna

The brief note that follows is the last letter that Anna wrote to her people in England after emigrating to Canada, for her parents had died.

When Anna left England, she anticipated that it was unlikely she would ever be reunited with her relatives there. But she made the best she could of it and tried hard to help her young family become good settlers. No matter what happened, she tried to find a bright side, and always, through her life, her trust in the rightness of God's decisions remained unshaken. She made a home for her family in the wilderness and filled young lives with her own unshakeable faith through many years of privation. Her reward was to live to see them carry on her ideals in homes of their own, making the later years of her own life peaceful and serene.

Coe Hill Mines/Wollaston/Febry 19th

My dearest Mother

How soon a year has rolled round since I last wrote to wish you many happy returns of your birthday. It will be soon the 3rd of March again! We all wish you many happy returns of the day.

How I wish the years as they come would find you better and stronger, but it is not our Father's will for you; I am sure He gives you strength to bear your heavy afflictions, or they would seem unbearable. I hope you are in your usual health. You will be glad, no doubt, when the spring comes and the weather will be a little brighter. How nice it would be if you could ride out, it would be such a change.

We are counting of the spring. I have been kept at home a great deal on account of the baby, not liking to take him out in the cold. We are all well, thank God. I was sick for a few days. I had what seemed like a return of the Grippe, but am all right again now. The children are looking well and growing fast. Baby is growing nicely. He is getting quite amusing, but has a very determined temper for a little thing. He has three teeth and another nearly through. He has lovely grey eyes, not like any of the others. We shall have one of our cows milking in a fortnight or so and then he can have all the new milk he likes, but he does not like eating. I have plenty of milk for him, and we shall soon have plenty of eggs for we have 28 hens and 2 cocks, or roosters.

We shall soon be sugar making again. I don't know how we shall get on, as I cannot leave the baby to go in the bush, and we shall miss Gertie. I will send you Gertie's last letter and you will see how she is getting on. Florence is quite well.

[Sister] Gertie has been to see me since I wrote last. She was looking very well indeed. We often some of us see her. I had a note from Harry last Saturday, he said they were both well. As soon as the weather is a little warmer, I think of going to see her and Mrs. Tivy. We have had a nice winter, plenty of snow. Today has been lovely, bright warm sunshine. The children play out with their sleighs and toboggans.

I hope Fanny and William are well. 'Tis a long time since we heard from them. We send our love to them, also to dear Rosa and Mary, and Father, hope he is well. I must send a short letter this time as I have no news. When I have been to see Gertie, I will tell you all about it.

You will think this a very short letter, but will do better I hope next time. With much love. Believe me, dearest Mother.

Yr loving Anna

With the building of the new house, Anna's pioneering days came to an end. The family were not considered prosperous, nor could they be thought of as poor. Each year saw fields expand, fences encircle them, and better crops grown to feed more stock. Buck and Bright, the slow-moving oxen, served their purpose well for a time and then were replaced by horses that accomplished more and could move at a better speed on the roads.

The old log barn became too small for the increasing crops, and a frame addition was put up to double its capacity. But through time, the woodsy humus supplying fertility to the soil gradually faded and manure had to be spread to replace its strength. Crops slowly got poorer and the stones to be picked off after each ploughing became more numerous. The farm work never grew easier, while David grew older and unable to accomplish as much as he had. The cheese factory, however, brought some ready money to the settlers. Small orchards were set out and flourished, supplying excellent apples without the frequent spraying that later became so necessary to guard the fruit against insects and disease.

The farm thus gave a comfortable living for quite a number of years until David and Anna grew older. Anna began to be troubled with the pains of rheumatism and the breathlessness of asthma. These afflictions limited her activities increasingly.

Gertie married into the Hewton family, Katy into the Tivys, while Florence chose a local blacksmith as her partner for life. Lily stayed single, as did Edward. Gertie and Lily taught school for a time, but Lily's health and gentle disposition were not suited to the work of preparing lessons and maintaining discipline. She took a secretarial course and worked for a few years in an office while devoting her leisure time to writing poetry.

When Gertie became a widow, she first moved to Trenton and then to the nearby village of Carrying Place, David and Anna spent their later years with her. Later on, Lily came to Carrying Place as well, while Katie and Florence settled not far away.

Frank married and took over the home farm. When war broke out in 1914 he joined up and was one of the early casualties. This left the old home place in the hills as a spot where nobody lived for any great length of time, though it still remained in the family.

David divided his time between looking after Gertie's garden and taking long and pleasant walks through the countryside. His cane and bushy white whiskers were well known through that area until he was well up into his eighties. Anna became more and more restricted in her movements and finally passed on. David lived hardly a year after she went.

The peaceful cemetery in Carrying Place is located on a rise of land where one can see eastwards the beautiful waters of the Bay of Quinte or westwards over that corner of Lake Ontario known as Weller's Bay. The site once was a resting place for Indians carrying their canoes and goods from one water to the other, hence the name of the village. It seems fitting that David and Anna should rest there on that rise of land, resembling the hills they had learned to love around the tiny shanty home in the great backwoods. Near Anna lie her four daughters. They are together again just as when their mother guided their lives in nearby Hastings County.

The Psalms were among Anna's favourite Bible readings. Of these, the 23rd with its assurance of peace and rest, and the 121st, that states "I will lift up mine eyes unto the hills from whence cometh my help" were the bulwarks of her faith that eventually God's plans for the world would come to pass in His own good time. Meanwhile, she is quietly waiting.